SO MANY LOVELY DAYS
The Greenwich Village Years

To Dona, with
much admiration
and appreciation.
May you have many,
many lovely days.
Mara

SO MANY LOVELY DAYS
The Greenwich Village Years

Mara Kirk Hart

Kirk Press
Duluth, Minnesota

So Many Lovely Days
The Greenwich Village Years

The best years are the first to flee.   Virgil

ISBN 978-0-9890478-0-7

Printed and bound in the United States of America
Book layout and design by Marlene Wisuri
Dovetailed Press LLC

Cover photograph by Consuela Kanaga, 1928
Butterfly graphic from *New Amsterdam Theatre* playbill, 1924
All photos are from the collection of Mara Kirk Hart.

Kirk Press
205 West Kent Road
Duluth, Minnesota 55812
marakirkhart@gmail.com

DEDICATION

To my beloved sister, Kitty

We possessed together the precious, the incommunicable past.
Willa Cather

Manhattan, 1999.   Photo: Jenny Bauer

Disclaimer ❧

Dear Reader,

Where I had facts, I used them and did not distort them. Where I had personal remembrances, I conveyed them as honestly as any faulty memory can. Where I had neither facts nor personal memories, I used imagination and tried to remain as true to George and Lucy, and the time and place, as I knew how. Where I re-imagined dialogue, I let you know. In all instances, although I have attempted to be as honest and as true to factual information as possible, I ask your indulgence, and take full responsibility for any omissions, distortions, or errors you may find in this book.

Mara Kirk Hart
December 2012

Acknowledgements ❧

I wish to offer profound thanks and gratitude to my wonderful writing sisters Gail Trowbridge, Terry Falsani, and Donna Schilling for their support, encouragement, comments, and careful reading of the manuscript during this long process. I offer heartfelt thanks to my dear friends Bob Saarela, Catherine Koemptgen, and Milan Kovacovic; my children and my memoir group, all of whom have been steadfast in their interest and encouragement.

Marlene Wisuri has my deepest appreciation for all visual and artistic aspects of this book. For that I offer her my profound thanks.

TABLE of CONTENTS

"Those were lovely exciting days. It was wonderful to be with the man I loved, to have a second-hand book shop in the Village, to be constantly making new friends."

Prologue: A Wonderful, Romantic Time

It is well past our bedtime, and the Andre champagne is now warm and flat. Mother and I are sitting on the gold couch in her Atlanta apartment. She's still in the blue dress she wore to her 90th birthday dinner at The Peasant, where she picked at her shrimp salad but greedily devoured the Baked Alaska. Wisps of her upswept hair are falling around her face, and her lipstick is smeared. "Let's have one of those candy bars," she says. Mother, once so discriminating, can no longer distinguish between Andre and Cliquot Brut champagne, between Mr. Goodbars and Godiva chocolates. I unwrap a Mr. Goodbar.

We're discussing—or rather I'm asking and Mother's answering—questions about the topic which has riveted my adult imagination, and about which I can never hear enough: my parents' first twelve years of marriage when they owned the Chelsea Book Shop in Greenwich Village. I am always hungry for time with Mother, for information about the shop, and—for that matter—always thirsty for champagne. "Those were lovely, exciting days," she says. "It was wonderful to be with the man I loved, to have a second-hand book shop in the Village, to be constantly making new friends."

Although I have heard these words many times, tonight I want more. If she loved Daddy so much, why was she unkind to him during most of my growing-up years? He drank a lot, yes, but probably wouldn't have if she'd treated him better. He's been dead for a quarter of a century, but I'm still trying to figure out their relationship. Tonight I'm ready for the truth. "And how did you and Daddy get along then?" I ask this tentatively, not sure I want to hear the answer, remembering her multiple threats of divorce.

"Oh, George was the handsomest, the kindest, the most loving husband I could possibly hope for. It was a wonderful, romantic time." I have to accept this. With even more trepidation, I move on to another painful subject: the births of my sister Kitty and me. Will she tell me again that they had wanted no children, or has she forgotten that, during these long years?

9

"And Kitty and me?"

Maybe it's the champagne, maybe it's her memory loss, maybe it's the rose-colored glasses she now wears, but Mother's story is different tonight. "Well, you weren't exactly planned. But then nobody planned in those days." She takes my hand: "You were as blonde as Kitty was dark. Adorable children. Oh, what would I ever have done without you two?"

After a sip of Andre, she continues: "We expected our whole life would be the bookshop and each other. How could we keep the shop and raise children too? After all, we usually slept till 10:00. But fate had it otherwise. Thank God." She still doesn't convince me. Even now, in my mid-fifties, sometimes I feel like an intruder, as if I were responsible for ruining their plans of a carefree life in the Village and for the closure of the book shop when I was still a child. Would they have been able to keep it without children? Would they have been happier? I smile and kiss her smooth cheek. "I love you," I say. And she tells me she loves me too. And at that moment I adore this frail, strong woman. I love hearing her speak so fondly of Daddy and of their early years of marriage. But are her memories "true?" Does it matter?

Soon Mother's eyelids start to droop. "Oh Mary, your mama is so tired."

Although I changed my name to Mara many years ago, Mother refuses to call me by anything other than my birth name. That's all right with me. We kiss goodnight, and we walk—my arm around her—to her bedroom.

"Want some help getting to bed?" She refuses, and I know she's too proud to accept.

Lucy Kirk at 90 in her Atlanta apartment with Bob Hart, 1988.

"Sweetheart, thanks for the delicious dinner," she hugs me tight. "I'll order that salad again."

I turn out the lights and crawl into bed next to my sleeping husband Bob. When Mother first met him she said: "Oh, honey, he reminds me so much of your father!" Much as I loved my father, I did not like to hear those words. Why was that? And recently the counselor I was seeing for anxiety asked me about Daddy. After my response, he said: "Your father taught you a lot, Mara. He taught you how *not* to be." Those words startled me. I vowed to change, to be more like Mother, to "warm both hands before the fire of life," to be valiant and optimistic, if possible. Someday, I think to myself, I'll try to sort out the facts of my parents' lives and make sense of reality. But when?

That night was over twenty years ago. It's taken this long to get enough distance from it all, to gain the right perspective. But can a daughter ever get the "right perspective" on her parents? I really don't know.

A few months later, in August 1988, Kitty and I took Mother to New York to continue her birthday celebration. We re-visited many places she and Daddy lived during their early years there, sat in the courtyard of their first apartment, and met with her old friend, Harvey Brewer, who had worked at the book shop for many years. Through the years, I kept asking Mother questions, and she answered as fully as she could. And after her death in 1994 I acquired her diaries.

I also have used the myth of the Chelsea Book Shop all my life. My myth has been this: "I grew up in Greenwich Village where my parents owned a second-hand book shop." This statement, particularly in Minnesota, never fails to draw exclamation points: "Wow! What a wonderful beginning!" Or "No wonder you love books!" And, of course this statement is true—as far as it goes. But it is only partially true. My parents closed the shop's doors forever before I was even six. And after that we no longer lived in the Village, but up on 123rd Street near Columbia, and then, when I was eleven, we moved to Pelham, New York, farther and farther away from the bohemian life that I longed to have as part of my identity.

According to the writer Nadine Gorimer, we write in order to make sense of life. Now, nearing my seventy-ninth year, I will try. This book, then, is my attempt to de-mythologize the early years of my parents' marriage and to make sense of their lives. And probably it's also an attempt to make sense of my life too, to forego the myth of my romantic growing up and to face reality. Am I ready to do this? I'm not sure.

PART ONE

SWELL TIMES

"Oh, he's okay. But here's my advice: never get out of bed before he does in the morning."

14

George and Lucy

I will begin at the beginning. My parents, (Ruth) Lucile Dvorak and George Willard Kirk met in October 1923, when Lucy was a reporter for the *Cleveland Press.* One day her friend Maxine Davis said: "Lucy, there's a charming new book shop in the Newman Stearns Building. The *handsomest* man you've ever seen runs it."

After work, Lucy, always interested in meeting handsome men, visited the bookshop and asked for James Branch Cabell's *Jurgen*, a book she assumed the attractive man wouldn't have. Her plan worked. George took her order, said he'd obtain a copy and deliver it to her. Just as she had hoped, he asked Lucy how he could contact her.

The next Friday afternoon, George arrived at the *Press* office, a copy of *Jurgen* tucked under his arm. They went out for coffee, he invited her to dinner on Saturday, and that was the beginning of a courtship which culminated in their engagement before Christmas, 1923. There was no ring; George didn't believe in that. Instead they exchanged gifts: he gave Lucy a pair of Lapis Lazuli earrings, and she gave George an inlaid chess set. That would become the pattern all their married life: for her something to wear, for him something to do. Pet names for each other were "Geordie" and "Lovin' Lu."

They were both 25, their personalities already well-formed, and they were both used to getting their own way. As a woman anxious to experience life, Lucy had no intention of staying home and taking care of others, as her mother had done. And George, although he left school after the eleventh grade, thought so highly of his intellectual abilities he scoffed when Lucy suggested further education for him: "If I knew more than I know now none of my friends would find me bearable." Who could teach him more than he already knew? Her tendency was to embrace the world; his tendency was to withdraw.

George saw no reason for a traditional marriage, since they loved each other and planned to have no children. He was moving to New York in August; after all, there was nothing to hold him in Cleveland. He had no relatives there except his brother Howard and his sister Helen. He loved one and didn't care much for the other. New York was where you had to be if you were a bookseller. Lucy should join him.

But no, not only did Lucy insist on marriage if they were to live together, she set three conditions for him to meet before the wedding: get his teeth fixed, pay his debts, and show that he could earn enough money to support himself and a wife. Thus another pattern established itself early in their relationship: Lucy making demands on him—sometimes reasonable and sometimes not—and George promising to comply, but not necessarily doing so.

The engagement proved to be long—over three years—and difficult, as they were separated during most of it: George establishing himself as a bookseller in New York, and Lucy remaining in Cleveland. During those years, George became close friends with Howard Lovecraft, Frank Belknap Long, and other writers of the supernatural. Eight of them, all poets and writers except for George, were all but inseparable, and formed the KALEM CLUB. He sent Lucy maps of Manhattan, raved about The Ziegfeld Follies, the theatre (especially *Iolanthe*,) Chaplin in *The Gold Rush*, the Egyptian exhibit at the Metropolitan Museum, the hikes in the New Jersey hills, the all-night walks, the interesting conversations, the many sights of New York, and oh, how she longed to join him there, to start a new life in the most exciting city in the world. But not until he had fulfilled his promises to her. He tried to fulfill them, but not too hard. He was used to talking and

"Rich and joyful entertainment. 'Iolanthe' must not be missed." —John Anderson in N. Y. Evening Post.

A postcard sent to Lucy from George in New York City, 1926.

A playbill sent by George to Lucy, 1925 or 26.

walking all night and sleeping all morning: "I am entertaining—and altogether too much—less than four hours of sleep a night," he wrote her.

They wrote each other about the books they were reading. Lucy read the moderns, and devoured the best-sellers as they came out: Hemingway's *In Our Time* and *The Sun Also Rises*; Dreiser's *An American Tragedy*; Ferber's *So Big*, and Lewis's *Arrowsmith*. George, with very few exceptions, read nothing that hadn't withstood the test of time. He wrote of Swinburne, Trollope, Dickens, Poe. For contemporary writing he admired only *The New Yorker*, which started publication in 1925, *Topper* by Thorne Smith, and *Imperial Purple* by Edgar Saltus.

In Manhattan, after working as a book scout, George owned shops in Chelsea (first on West 15th Street, and then on West 14th), and finally, in February 1927, a few weeks before his wedding, he opened the Chelsea Book Shop at 58 West 8th Street, Greenwich Village. He and Lucy were to own and operate this shop for the next twelve years.

GEORGE W. KIRK, *bookseller*, announces that he has removed his place of business from 1894 Charles Road to Room 416 The Newman-Stern Building, 1740 Twelfth Street corner Walnut, Cleveland, where he has on display a more extensive collection of books * * * In adding to his former stock special attention has been given to volumes of general interest, books on art, rare items and modern first editions. A representative collection of autographs is also being shown * * * A cordial invitation is extended to call and inspect the stock in the new quarters. Telephone Prospect 674.

George Kirk, bookseller, announcement, 1923.

Announcement of Chelsea Book Shop move to West 8th Street, 1927.

On and after
MONDAY, FEBRUARY 21st

The
CHELSEA BOOK SHOP
will be located at
58 WEST 8th STREET
Telephone Spring 6866

RARE BOOKS · FIRST EDITIONS · CIRCULATING LIBRARY
SECOND-HAND BOOKS · PRINTS

George, the youngest of three, was orphaned by twenty and married at twenty-one. By the time he met Lucy he was divorced, and already quite experienced in the book business. While still a teenager, he began work at Korner and Woods' bookstore in Cleveland. There he met Harriet Brooks, who became his first wife. After their marriage on January 31, 1920, George and Harriet moved to Berkeley, California, where they worked in the Arts and Crafts Bookshop of Paul Elder. It was from Paul Elder, almost thirty years George's senior, that he learned most about bookselling and publishing. In 1922, Mr. Elder—no one ever called him Paul—encouraged George to publish *Twenty-One Letters of Ambrose Bierce*, letters written to George's friend, Samuel Loveman, his one and only publication.

Lucy, on the other hand, was the eldest of three children, the apple of her parents' eyes. At seventeen she went to a fortune teller who told her she was going to experience everything there was in life. Lucy was thrilled. She graduated from Flora Stone Mather (the women's college of Western Reserve) with a degree in journalism, and although she had held various jobs, she was

Joseph Dvorak, Lucy's father, at his Czech-American drugstore in Cleveland, ca. 1930.

still living at home. She had been a publicity writer for the Cleveland School Board, a feature writer and school page editor for the *Cleveland Press*, and at the time of meeting George, she was a reporter on that newspaper. After their engagement, she became an advertising copywriter at McCann Erickson where she met Homer Haverhill, who became a life-long love. Although she was sorely tempted by Homer (and throughout her life occasionally voiced regrets that they had not married,) she remained true to George during their engagement. Homer and Lucy saw each other several times a year until his untimely death. Were they lovers? I'm not sure.

Lucile Dvorak dressed to ride a camel in the Barnum & Bailey Circus for the *Cleveland Press*, 1923.

After leaving McCann Erickson's, Lucy became a front agent for Chautauqua. She traveled much of the East Coast booking engagements in small towns, which allowed her to visit George in New York several times. Although in truth she couldn't wait to be with him, starting a new life there, she always returned to her parental home. After all, promises were promises, and George had promised. In preparation for her marriage, Lucy took cooking classes. Once she mailed muffins to George who—instead of praising them—joked about a terrible accident that occurred when he removed something hard and round from a package, which then fell to the ground and killed his cat (Edgar Evertson von Saltus Kirk).

Lucy was miffed, of course. No more packages.

Knowing that George had been married before, Lucy did some checking. She called his first wife to ask if there was any reason she shouldn't marry him, and received an interesting response: "Oh, he's okay," said Harriet. "But here's my advice: never get out of bed before he does in the morning."

Early on in their engagement, George wrote out their marriage vows and Lucy signed them. That was enough for George. But not for Lucy. No, she would only be with George when they could have a proper wedding in Cleveland, and when he had fulfilled her requirements. He did see a dentist a few times, but then he ran out of money. He tried—but not too hard—to pay off his debts, but they just kept mounting. Much as he may have wanted to be able to support her, he was unwilling or unable to work hard enough to do so. Lucy didn't have to know these things, at least not until after they were married.

At Christmastime 1926, when George visited her in Cleveland, he gave Lucy an ultimatum: either they marry early in 1927 or call the whole thing off. Lucy agreed: it had been too long. She set the date and the place: March 5, 1927, at Old Stone Church in Cleveland. "Three-five-seven," she said years later, "so George would never forget our anniversary date." But of course he often did.

For the Chelsea Book Shop

Walk into Chelsea where each street
    Climbs down to take a tug or wherry;
Never a rose-tree shall you meet,
    Never a lilac near the ferry.

By slip and spar and silhouette,
    The ancient ghosts cling each together;
The city streets are damp and wet ~
    They vow 'tis only mild, Spring weather.

Yet when the Winter, vast and pale,
    Beckons with snow and wind at riot;
They seek a shelter from the gale,
    Within your realm of books and quiet.

And see your shelves stand row on row,
    And hear the world move by with laughter~
More than the living ever know,
    The wisdom of the dead knows after.

~ Samuel Loveman

Poem by Samuel Loveman

Calligraphy by Rheinhart Kleiner

1925.

"Give us a broad smile:
for God's sake, man,
it's your wedding day!"

Never Shall We Be "Married"

Nobody believed in marriage anymore; certainly not George Kirk. And certainly none of his New York friends; that's why none of them came to Cleveland to attend his wedding. Of his friends, only Howard Lovecraft was married—and he wished he weren't. Since George and Lucy had already written their vows, and since they would have no children, he saw no sense in going through this silly ceremony. He'd already had one failed marriage. Wasn't that enough? But Lucy insisted, and since he loved her and wanted to be with her, he complied.

Okay, he'd oblige her by putting on the blue suit she'd rented for him, and the paisley tie she'd chosen, but nix on the top hat. He'd never worn a hat and never would. And why not his usual bow tie? He hated these long floppy ones that always dipped into the soup. Didn't she know that? Well, within hours they'd be married and then he'd bring her back to New York.

The night before he had boarded the train from Grand Central to Cleveland. After arriving this morning—Saturday March 5th, 1927 to be exact—he went straight to his brother Howard's to rest. He had hoped to nap until early afternoon, but Lucy phoned to say he needed to be at the church early to have his portrait taken. No, she wouldn't be there: it was bad luck to see each other before the wedding.

So here he was in the chapel of Old Stone Church, sitting for his formal portrait. If they had to marry, why couldn't they have kept it simple, and gone before a Justice of the Peace in Manhattan? He hated all this formality. He sure could use a stiff drink. Or two. He lit his pipe.

Years ago when he'd married Harriet they did it right. They just went down to the courthouse and told her parents afterwards. They'd had some good times, especially out in Berkeley working in Paul Elder's wonderful bookstore. He still couldn't understand why Harriet had wanted to divorce. Oh well, it didn't matter much now. Would he ever understand the mysteries of a woman's mind?

George was brought back from his reveries by the photographer's voice: "Take that pipe out of your mouth and put it on the table next to you. Give us a broad smile; for God's sake, man, it's your wedding day!" George put the pipe on the table, but no, he refused to smile. He didn't want to show his crooked teeth. He just never had had the time or the dough to get them fixed. "Okay then, just turn a little to the left. A little more. That's good. Now hold it there. Good."

It was after 3:30 and he could hear guests entering the damp, cavernous church. Why were churches always so depressing? And why in the world did Lucy choose the biggest and the oldest one in Cleveland, right here on Public Square?

She wasn't even religious. When he left home, after being strictly raised by a Presbyterian father and a Mennonite mother, he vowed never to set foot in a church again. He was surprised Lucy wanted something so formal; he thought she was more carefree, more casual than that. Well, if he had to jump through these silly hoops to be with her, he would.

Howard, who was his best man, steered George to the small waiting room behind the altar, took a flask from his pocket, and offered his brother a swig of whiskey, took one himself, and once more checked his pockets for the ring. God bless him. Howard was nervous these days too, since his wife was expecting their first child any day now. What would George have done without him? He wouldn't even be here if Howard hadn't lent him seventy-five plunkers for the trip.

The Old Stone Church, Public Square, Cleveland, where George and Lucy were married, March 5, 1927.

24

All was in order. The organ started up—something by Bach—and Howard led him out to the altar. The guests—hundreds of them it seemed—stood. Down the aisle came Helen Jones and Millie Arreda, Lucy's maid and matron of honor, followed by the ushers, Lucy's brothers Ray and Bill. Finally came his Lucy on her father's arm. Thank God she wasn't wearing one of those silly long gowns. Instead, she wore a beige dress, a short veil, had her hair piled up on top of her head the way he liked it, and carried a bouquet of white roses. She was even more beautiful than he remembered her, and she smiled all the way down the aisle. Not so her father: looking choked up and serious, he took Lucy to the altar, kissed her cheek, shook George's hand, and then, head bowed, joined his wife Ada in the front pew.

Howard nudged him and George stepped forward. And then they were exchanging those frightening, beautiful vows: "I, George Willard Kirk, take thee, Ruth Lucile Dvorak, to be my wedded wife, to have and to hold from this day forward...in sickness and in health...till death do us part."

Although these words meant little in comparison to their private contract, he said them without hesitation and without stammering. But what was that sound? He looked down and there was Lucy's mother Ada, sobbing, and Lucy's father Joe, sniffling and blowing his nose. Oh for god's sake, their daughter was almost thirty, yet they still treated her like a girl! But almost immediately he softened: Lucy was their beloved eldest child, their only daughter, and he'd be taking her away to New York. Really, who could blame them?

And then Lucy repeated her vows which, he was amused to note, included the word "obey." That would be the day! He had no trouble slipping the gold band on her finger. She didn't have to worry about a ring for him: he refused to wear one. And then they were pronounced "man and wife." He lifted her veil and they kissed. She smelled of lavender and tasted of peppermint, as always. He hoped the pipe tobacco masked the smell of whiskey. The organ started Mendelssohn's "Wedding March," Lucy took his arm, smiled up at him, and the guests stood once again, greeting the bride and groom as they walked back up the aisle.

Flanked by Howard, Lucy's parents, brothers, and bridesmaids, they received hugs and well wishes. Everyone complimented Lucy on her dress, and congratulated

George. After coffee and cookies in the church basement, Howard drove them to the Hotel Cleveland, where Lucy's parents hosted a wedding supper. Not George's favorite food—Chicken a la King and molded Jell-O salad. Lucy's father, who drank nothing stronger than beer, opened a bottle of champagne and shared it among the ten guests. George still wore the rented suit, but at least he had removed the silly tie and opened his shirt collar. Lucy seemed in her element, the center of attention, sitting at his right, calling him her "Geordie," kissing him, holding his hand under the table.

"My God, Lucy, where did you find all those people?" George asked as soon as they were alone. From George's side, there were two family members at the wedding: his brother Howard and his sister Helen; and two childhood friends, Howard Wolff and Jake Falstaff. His parents were long since dead. But Lucy had her parents, brothers, grandmother, aunts, uncles, cousins, and seemingly hundreds of friends. She laughed, and said she was disappointed that more people couldn't come.

It was close to 10:00 before they were in their hotel room. "Oh, wasn't everything just perfect?" Lucy said, hugging and kissing him. "Of course I wish Millie Dennison had been there, but her baby's due soon. Aside from that, the sunny day, that beautiful old church, my sweet family, the delicious dinner, and you, you were wonderful through it all."

Well, he certainly wasn't going to complain now! He wouldn't spoil the mood. Finally they'd be alone for the night, and could sleep in on Sunday as long as they wished. This time, Lucy would be relaxed. During their long engagement, when she had visited him in New York, she'd been tense, fearful of being discovered.

Sunday afternoon they took a taxi to Lucy's parents' house in Washington Park to say their good-byes. Lucy wore her new green coat with the fur collar. George wore his familiar tweed jacket, and left the suit for them to return to the rental company. He saw for the first time the piles of wedding presents: Franciscan Desert Rose dishes, Towle sterling, linens, vases, trays, my God, so much stuff! Lucy's parents were crying. So was she. George promised he'd take good care of their daughter, and that, for sure, they'd come back for Christmas. Lucy's brother

Bill drove the newlyweds down to Union Station, where they boarded the 7:00 p.m. train to Manhattan.

"Did you get us a drawing room?" asked Lucy.

"Girl, I never even thought of it," replied George. "I got us an upper and a lower." It was the first lie of his married life. Of course he'd thought of it, but he couldn't ask Howard for more money. And he couldn't tell Lucy how broke he was. He and Lucy would just have to manage.

The Creed of George Kirk and Lucile Dvorak

(Written by George, signed by Lucile, January 1924)

- The giving of commands will be unnecessary, for one will feel ashamed if the other has to express a desire.
- Never shall we be *married*.
- Love ever shall be our bond, marriage never.
- May trivialities never assume undue importance.
- May either be ready to ask forgiveness although certain that they are not in the wrong.
- May each always endeavor to accord with the mood and desires of the other.
- May neither consider it possible to lower themselves by submitting to any inclination or desire prompted by the love of the other.
- May the present be such that we may, together, look back upon this period without regrets, as the beginning of our everlasting love.

"I did and do love that charmed spot. So many delightful restaurants: The Jumble Shop and Alice McCollister's, and Gonfarowni's. And the many little restaurants (really speakeasies) which served wonderful food. You could always get a full meal until midnight in the area."

That Charmed Spot

The Empire State train carrying the newlyweds from Cleveland pulled in to Grand Central Station at 7:30 Monday morning March 7, 1927. Many years later Lucy said: "We were not sophisticated enough to get a drawing room, and had an upper/lower, but really didn't need the upper." George and Lucy collected their luggage from a redcap, and hailed a taxi to the Cornish Arms Hotel on West 23rd, where George had been living since he moved the book shop to 8th Street. The previous Chelsea Book Shops had actually been in Chelsea, where he had rented two-room apartments, first on West 14th Street and then one block north, using the front room as the shop and keeping the back one as his private quarters.

Here's how I imagine their first morning in New York together. Lucy was impressed by the Cornish Arms, just a year old and with amenities she loved: a soft bed, Chesterfield chairs, shiny metallic fixtures and a marble vanity. After checking in, more lovemaking, bathing, and changing their clothes, the handsome couple—George in his tweed jacket and Lucy in her green coat with the fur collar—walked hand in hand that chilly sunny morning, across 23rd to 5th Avenue. Lucy had finally arrived at her Mecca, the center of culture and art. Full of anticipation, anxious to begin her new life, she just couldn't wait to see the book shop.

They stopped for breakfast at Chock Full o'Nuts, where Lucy savored the deep fried donuts rolled in powdered sugar, the freshly-squeezed orange juice, and the rich coffee that George had raved about. They, like the other customers, sat at the counter. "What a wonderful beginning to our new life," smiled Lucy, brushing sugar from her coat. "I love you, Geordie," she added, kissing him on the cheek.

George caressed her thigh: "Lucy, I've dreamed about this time for years, and now it's finally here." He took her hand with the shiny gold band, and raised it to his lips. Then, lighting his pipe, he said, "Let's go, kid," and they resumed their walk.

It was a yellow world. On this early spring day, daffodils and forsythia were in bloom. Lucy's greedy eyes devoured it all: the Flatiron Building, where Broadway crossed 5th Avenue, the street vendors with roasted chestnuts and jumbo pretzels, the organ grinder with his monkey. At a florist's, George bought violets and pinned them on Lucy's lapel. As they walked south on 5th, George provided a running commentary, proud of his city and his neighborhood, happy to show it off to his bride. At 15th Street they stopped to examine the new Barnes & Noble store. Across 5th at 11th Street, he called her attention to the Brevoort Hotel. They continued down 5th toward the familiar arch, the entrance to Washington Square Park, and took a right on 8th Street.

They were happy. So what if the book shop was no longer in Chelsea? So what if George's dental work wasn't completed yet? After all, he had done all he could so far. At least, thought Lucy, he had paid his debts and was supporting himself. And it *was* expensive to live in New York.

Arm in arm they walked across 8th towards 6th Avenue, past The Whitney Museum, Damroch's, Denbly's Drugstore, Sutter's bakery, the Jumble Shop, and

The Jumble Shop

Julia Kittner's antique store. "Very soon, Lucy," he squeezed her waist. She could clearly envision the shop he was so proud of. He had written her about it: "I desire that the atmosphere of the CBS be precious. My personal taste would be to make it cheery— the shelving and woodwork will be a light cream—the walls a light yellow—no, I dunno, tan perhaps. Am not yet fully decided *re* furnishings. A couple of bookcases. Either a settee or a sofa or large table to dominate with everything to radiate from that....Had a number of pictures framed and I like them much. I like my taste, and am almost always sorry when I follow another's advice."

Lucy loved the romance of marrying a bookish man and living in Greenwich Village. Although she had so hoped she could run the shop with him, George had explained that, as of now, Eddie Lazare was his assistant, and he could afford no more.

It was almost noon when they reached the Chelsea Book Shop at 58 West 8th Street, a narrow doorway on the south side of 8th, wedged between the antique store and a shoe repair shop. George fumbled in his pocket for the key: "Well, here we are, sweetheart, and there's my Edgar in the window," he grinned with pride, no hint of shame or regret, as he opened the door. (George had written her about Edgar: "Oy! The darlingist kitten vot I've adopted! His name is Edgar Evertson von Saltus Kirk and oy! You otta see him! What a joy he is to me!") Lucy was prepared for the cat, but certainly not for the shop. Her jaw dropped, and her smiling face turned to disbelief: "This is IT? You're kidding me!"

Immediately she was sorry for these words. She didn't know what to say now, taking in this tiny dark storefront, the cat sleeping in the window among books scattered randomly, no order or neatness, seemingly hundreds of cartons filling the narrow floor space. Lucy, not wanting to hurt her new husband, fought back feelings of outrage, of being duped. It was in stark contrast to what she had

George Kirk in front of the Chelsea Book Shop, July 1930.
Photo: Herman Seid of the *Cleveland Press*.

anticipated—definitely not love at first sight. She had expected cream bookcases surrounding a sofa and a large table.

But then Lucy thought, after all, George had moved here only two weeks earlier. What could she expect? And, as she always did, she rallied. "I can make something of this," she thought. And so she would.

First they needed a place to live. At that time, the Village was going through much remodeling, converting slum-like five-story walkups to attractive small apartments, each with a fireplace. Within a week they rented a newly-remodeled 4th story walk-up apartment above the book shop for $65 a month. It consisted of a fair-sized room with a fireplace, a kitchenette, and a bath: clean and easy to care for. They bought a double bed and retrieved the couch, blue reading chair, wooden table, chairs, and pipe stand that George had stored with his former landlady, Ma Eisart. Until Ada mailed their wedding presents, they made do with George's table-ware and linens from Woolworth's. Lucy wrote her mother: "I made the most god-awful two pairs of curtains by hand. I am quite proud of them."

One day that first week, George's assistant Eddie took Lucy aside and told her a hard truth: because George could not afford to pay his salary of $25 a week, he was looking for other work. Part of Lucy was chagrined by this news, but part of her was pleased. She *could* work at the shop after all. This had been her dream.

And so they settled in and worked hard to get the book shop presentable and ready to re-open. George painted the walls cream. He built cases, painted them a light yellow, and lined the walls with floor to ceiling books. Lucy washed the windows, arranged the space tastefully, fixing a comfortable bed for Edgar, and she scrubbed and waxed the floor. She bought chairs at the Salvation Army and painted them turquoise, her favorite color. On the counter, in addition to the cash register and the Royal typewriter, they had a roll of brown wrapping paper, twine, scissors, paper clips, and scrap paper. Behind the counter they had a shelf labeled "R.S." ("real stuff," according to George). Here they kept books which had been prohibited for sale in the U.S., including Joyce's *Ulysses*. On the back wall of the shop they hung lithographs of Poe, Stevenson, and Hawthorne. Lucy hung a bright curtain behind the counter to hide the "stockroom," which had a washbowl, toilet, and a fireplace. She bought a used couch and a coffee table for their private space behind the curtain. They set the book shop hours as noon to 11:00 p.m.

Lucy's presence there brought about changes, and not all of them to George's liking. For one thing, she took charge of the money and insisted they keep meticulous financial records. He had kept track neither of income nor expenses, and was used to dipping into the till for whatever he needed or wanted: a book, a movie, a meal, a beer or two. She set their joint salary at $50 a week. If George ran out of money by week's end, well, too bad. He'd just have to wait a few days. Until now George had seen only the carefree Lucy that he loved; he wasn't too sure about this practical side of her.

Because of their long mornings, and remembering Harriet's admonition ("Never get out of bed before he does"), Lucy insisted that George bring her coffee in bed every morning. After coffee, I can envision Lucy wearing her flowered robe, smelling of Yardley's lavender soap, her long hair loose, making her favorite breakfast: bacon and eggs, Thomas's English Muffins, orange juice, and coffee with lots of cream. While they sat on the spindle-backed chairs at the black drop-leaf table, set with Desert Rose plates and sterling, Lucy would want to talk, but George would be hidden behind a book, maybe Trolloppe, Dickens or Poe.

One Saturday morning in June they broke their routine, and walked over to 5th Avenue to watch the historic Lindbergh parade. The ceremonies were held right there, at the base of the Washington Arch. It was thrilling, wrote Lucy, to see handsome Charles Lindbergh, the American hero, who had just returned from the first solo flight across the Atlantic. And in late August they changed their morning routine again. Instead of sleeping in, they joined the huge crowd marching down Fifth Avenue wearing black arm bands to protest the unjust executions of Sacco and Vanzetti. One evening they were amazed to see the new moving electric sign at Times' Square. They saw the musical *Showboat*, and the Marx brothers' film, *Cocoanuts*, and loved them both.

Even with the shop's wonderful location, its newly decorated space, its enthusiastic and attractive owners, book sales seldom brought in the anticipated $50 a week. Lucy pondered: what to do? How could they earn more money? She settled on the idea of expanding the circulating library, and decided to take full charge of it. Why a circulating library? In the early part of the 20th Century, public libraries, at least in New York, were meant for research. If any books circulated, they were the classics. If a patron wanted to read a contemporary book or a best-seller, she had two choices: either buy it or borrow it from a lending (circulating) library.

These libraries were common throughout the United States. They required a membership, which meant a small deposit; charged a nominal overnight fee, and a set amount per day after that. Lucy set the membership fee at $5, charged $1 deposit per book, 10¢ per book overnight, and after that 3¢ per book per day. She set up a window display, and reserved a few shelves at the front of the shop for her library. She printed monthly brochures of new books available, and began a card file with information about each customer.

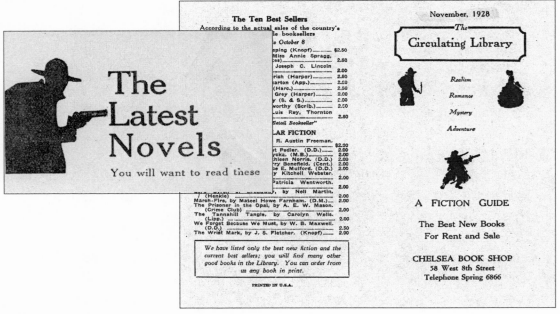

Lucy ordered all the new books. Although most of them came from either Baker & Taylor or The American News Company, several reviewers, after getting books free from the publishers, sold them to her for half price. Thus everyone profited. Two of these reviewers became their friends: John Chamberlain, who later achieved fame as a radio and TV announcer, and Hershel Brickell, the literary editor of the *New York Post*.

The library became a great success. Several customers read a book a day. It brought in many new customers who then browsed and bought book shop stock. In this way too, since the shop sold only used and rare books, Lucy was able to read the current best sellers: *Elmer Gantry, The Bridge of San Luis Rey, Lady Chatterley's Lover,* and *Look Homeward, Angel* among others. After some months, these books became part of the book shop's stock.

George cared not a whit about new books, and at first had great reservations about the library. He decried commercialism, which he labeled as "Babbittry" and believed books had to withstand the test of time—at least thirty years—to be worth reading. Aside from Yeats, Joyce, and Saltus, his literary taste extended no further than the 19th century, and he preferred even earlier authors: Chaucer, Shakespeare, Marlowe, Wordsworth, and Coleridge. Although he had to thank Lucy for the library's success, and appreciated the additional income, he would have nothing to do with it.

Prohibition helped with sales also, and was one reason the shop stayed open until 11:00, when others had long since closed. Whenever the police raided the Jumble Shop (a speakeasy down the street) some customers came over to the book shop and appeared to be casually browsing. In their inebriated state they often bought books. This is how George and Lucy met several of their friends, including Eddie Bierstadt and his wife Catherine MacKenzie, both writers for the *New York Times*.

Prohibition never achieved its purpose, as, in addition to bootlegging and speakeasies, many people made what they called "bathtub gin," meaning they brewed alcoholic concoctions in their bathtubs. (To give you an idea of the insurmountable job the police had in controlling alcohol consumption, in 1925 there were over 50,000 speakeasies in New York City alone.) Lucy recalled that she and George brewed saki in this way: "3-5-9-12 in that order for the ingredients: that's three cups of rice, five cups of raisins, nine cups of sugar, and twelve cups of water. It was potent stuff. We brewed it for six weeks in the bathtub, and then put it in a huge crock to steam it. Then we invited friends over."

Although they were getting by financially on library income and book sales, Lucy decided they should rent a cheaper apartment. And so in October 1927 they moved to a garden apartment at 53 West 11th Street. It had a shared bath, so the rent was only $55 a month. As Lucy recalled: "It was a railroad apartment—living room with a fireplace, darkish 'office,' and a kitchen. The kitchen was repainted for us the next St. Patrick's day by an Irishman who used a vivid, violent green paint!" One evening, with the paint smell too strong to stay at home, George and Lucy went to see Al Jolson in *The Jazz Singer*, the first ever talking movie. They weren't sure they liked hearing words spoken instead of having them projected on the screen. With the rent money saved, Lucy bought a chest of drawers from Goodwill for $60. (I now have this chest in my writing room.)

One night during a quarrel that first fall, Lucy flung her wedding ring from the bed, vowing never to wear it again. And although, of course, they had made up by morning, she never did. Try as they might, even pulling up some floorboards, they never found the ring.

The lost ring caused an immediate problem. When they visited Cleveland at Christmastime Lucy certainly couldn't go without a wedding ring. How would she explain? So George ordered a replacement ring "on credit" from their neighbor and jeweler friend, Jo Michaels. He would pay what he could monthly from the meager allowance Lucy allotted him. Jo Michaels made an intricate gold ring set with five topazes, George's birth stone, which Lucy wore the rest of her life. (I wear it now.)

But before Christmas came Thanksgiving, Lucy's first holiday apart from her parents. They invited Eddie Lazare to dinner, and Lucy made a typical Czech meal: pork roast with sauerkraut, dumplings, and roasted potatoes. After it was in the oven they walked to Washington Square Park to enjoy the sunny day. But once there, Lucy became homesick, and cried and cried. George and Eddie had no idea what to do, and try as they might to console her, nothing worked. Although eventually she calmed down and they shared a delicious meal, all her life Lucy recalled this as the first and only time she was homesick.

Anyway, Lucy knew they'd be in Cleveland for Christmas, with Eddie keeping the shop open during their absence. She saved for the train fare and expected George to do the same, even though he was also making payments on the ring. Although she repeatedly reminded him not to loan money at this season, he did. He lent $5 to "a tearful chap" who never returned it. And so Lucy, angry and unhappy, had to borrow money for their tickets. On *this* overnight trip I imagine they needed both the upper and the lower berths. They stayed with Lucy's parents and her brother Bill, still at home. And with her new husband, surrounded by family love, I'm sure Lucy was happy once again.

We get an outsider's view of their relationship from Howard Lovecraft, divorced and living in Providence. In May 1928, during a visit to New York, Lovecraft wrote to his beloved Aunt Lillian: "Kirk—good old Georgius—whose marriage has proved extremely congenial, and who is still the same happy-go-lucky, unsubdued old nighthawk of yore….He has a basement flat on West 11th Street—separate from his shop and circulating library on West 8th, although he lived over the latter at first. Kirk, honest old Mac [Everett McNeil,] and I walked down Broadway together, and when we came to the elevated at 66th, Kirk insisted that Mac and I hop on and accompany him home for a further session. We did so, and found Mrs. Kirk half-expecting such a codicillary assemblage. She is a pleasant blonde person, not especially young or good-looking, but apparently a highly congenial partner for the carefree and irresponsible Georgius. The household served tea, crackers and cheese." Congenial as George and Lucy seemed to Lovecraft, they were often disappointed and exasperated with each other. They loved each other, yes, but financial problems prevented the hoped for marital bliss. What to do?

Lucy decided seasonal greeting cards would bring in more money. And so, by November 1928, much to George's dismay, a well-stocked rack of Christmas and Hanukah greetings dominated the shop's central space. Lucy ordered cards from Rustcroft, Hallmark, and the American Greeting Cards Company; and several local artists—Tirzah Perfect, Putnam Strong, and Myron and Florence Parrott—offered cards on consignment.

The holiday cards were so successful in 1928 that Lucy replenished the stock for Valentine's Day and Easter. And so from November to April the card rack dominated the book shop's center. Lucy was proud of her selections, and George, much as he grumbled about "Babbittry," couldn't help but appreciate the income they brought in. Here's a story: year after year a customer came in to buy Valentine cards. He searched the stock and finally picked out a 5¢ card and a dollar card—boxed and lacy, with a sachet enclosed. At the cash register he said: "One for my wife and one for my sweetheart." He then handed Lucy the expensive card, kissing her on the cheek, and took the 5¢ card home to his wife.

38

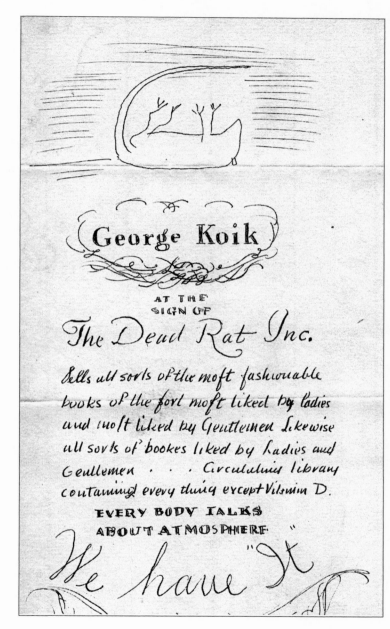

"He was an enormous man, but he was a pushover."

Other People

"We loved our customers and our customers loved us," Mother recalled. "Your father looked so handsome in his tweed jacket." It's true, I believe, that they did love most of their customers and the bookshop had a loyal following. But they didn't love them all, nor did all the customers love them.

I was disappointed to learn that my beloved poets Edna St. Vincent Millay and e.e. cummings were not among their customers, since they both lived in the Village at that time. However e.e. cummings' mother was a frequent visitor. In truth, much of the famed literary life of the Village had left by the late 1920s—many of the writers going abroad—especially to Paris—because of prohibition and censorship. Already come and gone from the Village were Sherwood Anderson, Willa Cather, Stephen Crane, John Dos Passos, Theodore Dreiser, Max Eastman, Marianne Moore, Eugene O'Neill, Man Ray, Edmund Wilson, Thomas Wolfe, and Elinor Wiley.

There were, however, a few literary customers. Among them was Thorne Smith who, after many hungry years, achieved success with his Topper books. Lucy remembered him as a very funny man and a very heavy drinker. Both the poet Kenneth Patchen and the playwright Eli Siegel were customers. Maxwell Bodenheim, who was dubbed "The King of Bohemia" and was often arrested for vagrancy, frequented the shop. Sometimes they saw him in a diner ordering only water and pouring ketchup in it for his lunch. George slipped him a few dollars whenever Lucy wasn't looking. Erskine Caldwell was a mail order customer. Eddie Bierstadt, a pioneer radio script writer and newspaper columnist, and his wife Catherine McKenzie, a childcare columnist for *The New York Times* were customers and friends.

In addition to John Chamberlain and Hershel Bricknell, Karl Decker—a Hearst correspondent for the Spanish American War—and Carl Carmen, Lyle Saxon, and Joseph Raznic were good customers also, and all—according to Lucy—"outstanding newspaper men."

A few celebrities were customers too; most notable of them was Houdini. He lived near the book shop George had previously owned on West 14th, and remained a customer at this new location. Also there was William Stephenson who became a well-known Canadian Arctic Explorer, using his Icelandic name "Viljalmur Stefannson."

The artists Charles Howard and Hester Miller were customers, as were the book designers Elizabeth McKinsty and Margaret Freeman. Consuela [Connie] Kanaga, the photographer, became a close friend. Margaret Freeman also worked at times for the book shop, and later she generously loaned George and Lucy her garden apartment.

Not famous but fascinating were Rheinhart Kleiner and John "Papa" Corell. Kleiner was George's friend from the Kalem Club and according to Harvey Brewer, "a gentleman of the old school and an irrepressible book collector. His manners and flowery speech seemed distilled from Dickens." Corell, "an eccentric and charming man," collected old printing presses and typefaces. He published an occasional booklet called *The Idler* made up from ornaments and cuts culled from old type specimen books, with maxims and quotations added any which-way in the margins. On several occasions he and his wife invited George and Lucy to their home in Armenia, New York, where the lawn was strewn with old millstones.

Here are a couple of stories about customers with whom there was no mutual love. Dr. Fralick, a frequent customer, was a cadger. He took something from the shop each time he came in: paper clips, sheets of paper, twine. One day as he was cutting some twine for himself Lucy said: "Put that *down* and stop taking *our* things!" Caught in the act, he mumbled loud enough for all to hear, "No *wonder* they murder bastard women!" Amazingly, he remained a customer for many years. We'll hear more about him later.

And then there was Herbert French, the anthologizer. He was in the book shop almost every day, and George and Lucy considered him a friend. Once however, when he went on vacation, he asked George if his mail could be sent directly to the shop during his absence. George said that would be fine. But no mail came for Mr. French. On his return, he accused George of stealing it. George laughed, but Lucy was indignant at this false accusation: "You can just leave, and *never* come back!" She kept berating him until he turned purple with anger and shouted: "You, you, you woman of Babylon!" Lucy laughed and shoved him out the door. "He was an enormous man," she said, "but he was a pushover." They never saw Mr. French again.

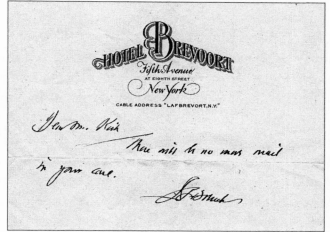

A note to George Kirk from Mr. French following the mail incident.

And then there were the employees. "Everyone wanted to work for us," Mother said, and that's probably not much of an exaggeration. George, although introverted and bookish, was easy-going and kind. Lucy was outgoing and friendly. Both were generous and humorous. The book shop atmosphere was casual and they encouraged browsing and conversation. Surrounded by used books, with kind employers, who wouldn't want to work there?

By fall 1927, Eddie Lazare returned to work part time, and remained a beloved and trusted friend and employee until the shop's closure in 1939. In the spring of 1928 Harvey Brewer, a young man still in knee-pants, came to work also. After high school graduation, Harvey worked full-time in the book shop for the next twelve years, and became a lifelong friend. I will get back to these two men, but first want to mention a few other employees through the years.

Barry McCarthy, a charming man according to Mother, liked to work when George and Lucy were at dinner. It was many months before they realized that Barry dipped his fingers in the till when he was alone in the shop, and they had to let him go. Although they lost money during Barry's employ, they gained great rewards in knowing his photographer wife, Consuela Kanaga. I will get back to her also.

Mother mentioned several others whom they employed over the years, adding pithy comments. Here are a few: Joseph Cox and Joanne Keener: "Both too nondescript for me to remember much." John Holman: "A handsome young twenty-four year old." Bill Crane: "He had a frigid wife." And three women, all of whom became family friends: Annette Smith, Bunny Hutchins, and Mary Tobin.

Back to Eddie Lazare. Eddie was in his late teens when he and George met in 1924, soon after George's arrival in New York. He helped George at his former book shops on 15th and on 14th, and he helped George move his stock to West 8th in 1927. After working part-time on and off at the shop, Eddie had a very successful career. He and his wife Ramona first edited *American Book Prices Current* and then *The American Bookman*, both "Bibles" of the rare book trade. They remained life-long friends.

And Harvey Brewer. One day, when Harvey was in his early twenties, a young woman wearing a chipmunk coat came into the shop. Although her name was Alice, George immediately dubbed her "Chippie." And Alice kept coming back. Many years later, Harvey related: "Alice recalls her mother inquiring why she made such frequent visits to the book shop. Was it that tall, dark, very handsome man? Nope, it was me."

Harvey and Alice married within the year. He was funny and very kind; Alice, slim and kind also, was a fine pianist and an avid bird watcher. They had no children and were a close, contented couple. After the book shop closed, Harvey opened a mail order business and later a shop in Closter, New Jersey, specializing in art books, art prints, and maps.

And of course George and Lucy had many friends. Lucy mentioned several who we never knew as a family, but I will pass on their names: Mary Bray, Margaret and Eleanor Belk, Catherine Cornell, Lyle Saxon, George Tichenor, Hugh Childers and his partner Alice Hurtilsbe, Jarvis and Lolita Fairchild, Walter and Olive Fischer, the Deckers, the Macbeths, and finally Bill and Florence Griffith, who invited them to vacation on Swan Island off the coast of Maine.

Friends Bob Spear and Margaret Harrison, and Al and Ruth Freeman hosted our family at their country homes for extended visits. Connie Kanaga photographed George and Lucy in their Village apartment in 1928. During the summer of 1937, in exchange for room and board at the Delaware Water Gap, she made a series of portraits of Kitty and me. Later Connie was mentored by Alfred Stieglitz, and achieved modest fame. She had a photograph included in his wonderful book *The Family of Man*.

Foremost among the friends who I remember well was Aunt Scottie. About a year after Lucy's marriage, her college friend Scottie (Helen Jo Scott) and her husband Bob Mann moved to New York. Scottie taught at New York University and Bob edited the periodical *Editor and Publisher*. The two couples were very close until Bob's sudden death in the late 1930s. Scottie helped George name me, and "gave me" her Hallowe'en birthday since mine was on Christmas Day.

On my tenth birthday she took me to the Waldorf for tea. That afternoon we had an important conversation. She said: "Mary, there are three kinds of people in the world: those who make things happen, those who let things happen, and those who ask 'what happened?' Your mother makes things happen. Your father asks 'what happened?' What kind of person do you want to be?" Of course I wanted to be a person who made things happen. This took a long, long time.

Scottie's life remained intertwined with our family, but her relationship with me, which had once been close, soured during my college years. In the mid 1950s, when Kitty and I attended Miami University in Ohio, Scottie was the director of alumni publications there. She told my roommate Lorraine about my parents: "Her mother's a wonderful woman, but her father's a drunken bum." These words infuriated me. How could Aunt Scottie, who pretended to love Daddy, speak of him in this way? After that, I never said a kind word about her. Although I was only nineteen at the time, I can't promise I would act differently today.

And then, finally there were the O'Neil's. Bill, an "advertising man," designed the logo for the Chelsea Book Shop. He was a large, red-faced man, good-natured and funny. Myrtle was quiet and kind. We girls were very fond of them. Although the close friendship between the two couples lasted many years, it ended abruptly and violently. Here's what happened. One night during a dinner party, when Kitty and I were about ten and eight, Bill came into our bedroom and sexually molested both of us. Kitty called Momma, who rushed to our room and realized what had happened. "God Damn you Bill, you *louse*, you sneak, how *dare* you touch my girls, you good for nothing bastard! Get out, just get out. I never want to see your ugly face again!" She pummeled him with her fists, and he slunk out without a word. Momma cradled us in her arms: "Oh my poor babes, my poor, poor babes. Are you all right?"

And they only saw each other again once. Years later Momma and I were walking down Madison Avenue when she spotted Bill O'Neil across the street. Disregarding the traffic, she ran across, and saying not a word, slapped him hard across the face. Then she turned and walked back to me.

Chelsea Book Shop logo designed by Bill O'Neil

"Lady, I wouldn't touch this with a ten foot pole.
Now you two just go home and make up."

Officer, Officer, Arrest This Man!

In late summer 1929 the Chelsea Book Shop was robbed. At that time the Village was safe, and few locked their doors at night. According to Lucy, nobody had much money, and so they all tried to help each other out. The stock market crash would come in October, and then nothing would be safe. But even before the crash, there was a difference between leaving your apartment unlocked when you were in it and leaving a shop unlocked when you were away. George felt justified in trusting people, but Lucy felt this trust was careless and foolish. Better safe than sorry.

I know the bare outlines of the robbery: George was alone in the shop when a man entered, saying George had a phone call next door. When George went to answer it, the shop was robbed. Here's how I imagine it to have been.

One sunny, sleepy Friday afternoon, with a hot wind blowing, George was selecting books for the five cent cart he'd put out Saturday morning. He had dismissed Eddie because business was slow. Edgar was dozing in the warm window. Lucy was home in their garden apartment on West 11th Street beginning dinner preparations. He tried to catch whatever breeze there was coming in the open front door. He'd close the shop at five; take the week's profits—such as they were—to Banca Commerciale Italiana on 6th Avenue, and then maybe stop for a beer. He felt

IN FULL SETTLEMENT OF ACCOUNT AS SHOWN BELOW IF INCORRECT PLEASE RETURN AT ONCE		**CHELSEA BOOK SHOP** 58 WEST 8TH STREET	NO. **1585** **2**
DATE	AMOUNT	NEW YORK, N.Y. _____ 193 ___	
		P̶AY TO THE ORDER OF _____ $ _____	
TOTAL		_____ **DOLLARS**	
LESS %DISCOUNT		COLLECTIBLE AT PAR THROUGH THE FEDERAL RESERVE BANK OF NEW YORK	
		BANCA COMMERCIALE ITALIANA **TRUST COMPANY** 1-752	
TOTAL DEDUCTIONS		SIXTH AVENUE OFFICE 339 SIXTH AVENUE	
AMOUNT OF CHECK		NEW YORK, N.Y.	
NO RECEIPT NECESSARY		_____	

lucky their bank remained open when so many had closed—well over 2,000 already! There was very little activity out on 8th Street; a few passers-by, someone washing a store window, another sweeping the sidewalk. He wondered what Lucy would make for dinner. He hoped it would be his favorite summer meal: steak from Gristede's, Lucy's potato salad, sliced tomatoes and cucumbers, and maybe some of that good bread from Sutter's. Their friends Scotty and Bob Mann were coming over. Dinner would be around 7:00, so they'd have time for a couple of martinis first.

He and Lucy had been getting along swell since he'd laid down the rules to her: don't curb me in, don't ask where I've been or where I'm going, don't be jealous, don't criticize me for drinking. He had to admit she was trying hard, and he loved her for that. She too had her rules, of course: watch every penny, don't be so generous, don't be so trusting, always put me first, be kind and gentle with me. And he also was trying his best. It was easy to be kind to Lucy. Gay, optimistic, smart, and—best of all—she was loving towards him.

The bell above the door rang. Finally a customer! George turned to see a young man, who seemed in haste: "You have a phone call next door," he said, pointing to the right. George, sensing an emergency, left immediately for the shoe repair shop. His sister? His brother? God forbid, Lucy? But next door Joe, the shoemaker, seemed puzzled. There had been no call for George, and why, anyway, would someone call there when the book shop had its own phone?

Puzzled and somewhat confused, George shook his head. How could he have forgotten that? How stupid could he be? He liked Joe, "an affable chap," so they chatted a few minutes before George returned to the shop. When he walked back next door, the shop was in more disarray than he'd realized: receipts, bookmarks, and flyers were blowing around. He straightened it up as best he could, still shaking his head at the strangeness of the phone call.

The bell jingled again, and an elderly man wandered in, "just to look around," he said, but then he spotted a book on the sale table. He brought it up to George, handing him a dollar. George opened the till for change, and swore beneath his breath, teeth clenched: "Damn!" The cash drawer lay mute and empty. He handed the book and the dollar back to the customer: "Just take it," he said. "Everything else is gone." It had been a relatively good week—probably $70 in profits—enough to pay him and Lucy their $25 each, and with some left over for groceries. But now nothing.

With his head hung low, George put out food and water for Edgar, and turned the key in the lock. He hung the sign on the door: "Open Tomorrow at Noon." Oh, how he hated the short walk to their apartment. He didn't even feel like stopping for beer. What would Lucy say? She'd call him a fool and a bungler. Well, at least he had some time. He wouldn't tell Lucy until after Scottie and Bob left. Maybe she'd be in a loving mood then. But certainly not for long. Good-bye to all thoughts of a peaceful evening.

And I'm sure these thoughts were not far from wrong.

The money was never recovered, and the thief never found. George was unable to give the police an accurate description of the robber. After that Lucy insisted George lock the shop whenever he left it unstaffed, and he did so—at least usually.

Even before the robbery, George and Lucy were just scraping by. George would willingly have gone into debt, but Lucy wouldn't hear of it, and Lucy was in charge of the finances. Once again, much to her chagrin, they had to borrow money to get through. But she put her foot down: no more spending money for George, no more stopping for drinks on the way home, no more steak dinners, and less eating out.

George, unhappy with these austerity measures, longed for his pre-marital freedom. So at times he took this freedom, which Lucy could not withhold from him, and was lax about getting home "on time." After all, a chap had to maintain some measure of independence!

Once, after staying out most of the night ("Met a chap and we played checkers,") and after quarreling about it the next day at the shop, they continued their quarrel on the walk home. Lucy, furious at George's refusal to apologize, saw a policeman across the street and hailed him over: "Officer, officer, arrest this man! He's harassing me!"

The policeman crossed the street and came to them. What did he see? A slim, pretty woman with her hair parted in the middle and pulled back into a severe bun. She was angry, all right. And he saw a smiling tall dark-haired man wearing a tweed jacket, smoking a pipe. "Are you harassing this lady?" he asked George.

"Nope, she's harassing me, officer."

The officer glanced at Lucy's wedding ring: "Are you two married?"

Did he wink at George as he asked this? George affirmed that yes indeed, they were married, for now anyway.

"Lady, I wouldn't touch this with a ten foot pole," the policeman said. "Now you two just go home and make up." When he left, George, the victor, couldn't stop laughing, while Lucy, angrier than ever, pummeled his arm all the way home. And then?

And then there was the real arrest. My childhood was clouded by the knowledge that before I was born my father had been in prison. I didn't know why, but I speculated a lot. Had he robbed a bank? Probably not, because he scolded me when I stole that candy bar from Woolworth's. Killed a man? Although I had seen him lop the head right off a copperhead, I couldn't imagine this gentle man who I loved so much doing anything seriously wrong, and yet....I didn't want to hear anything bad about him, and so was afraid to ask. What in the world could he have done to warrant time in jail?

My parents enjoyed playing up the arrest with varying stories of his escape. One story was that George became friends with the prison guard and they made a deal: George traded his beautiful pocket knife for an unlocked gate. Another story: Lucy baked an apple pie for him, and hidden in the pie was a file. After using the file as a saw, months and months later, he finally broke through the prison bars to freedom. This story was my preferred favorite, romantic and heroic. Many years later Mother related this story, which I assume to be true.

In late 1929 they bought a used model T Ford with a rumble seat. George was delighted to own this, the first car of his married life: it represented freedom, a concept he held in the highest esteem. At that time about one in five Americans owned a car, and he wanted one too. Lucy cared nothing for cars, never learned to drive, and remained a frightened, nervous passenger all her life. So George often drove alone.

Because they needed a garage and there were none to be had in the Village, George and Lucy moved to "a lovely, big, two room apartment with a garage" at 632 Van Cortland Avenue in Yonkers, and drove to the book shop daily. George drove to auctions and estate sales on Long Island, Staten Island, New Jersey (using the newly-opened Holland Tunnel) and even to Pennsylvania, bringing home purchases in his car.

On one such occasion, in the spring of 1930, George was pulled over by a policeman on Riverside Drive. "Do you know what the speed limit is here?" the officer asked. George wasn't sure. "Do you know how fast you were going?" George wasn't sure of this either. "This is a warning. The next time, a hefty fine or time in the brig. Do you understand?" George nodded, smiled politely, thanked the officer, and happily drove on, amused by the incident. Something to tell Lucy about.

But Lucy was not amused and said something like: "It's really not funny at all. We can't afford a fine, and you know it. Just take it easy, obey the law, and we won't have any trouble."

A few days later it happened again. George, returning to Manhattan from a sale in New Jersey, had just crossed the George Washington Bridge. And guess what? Same place and same policeman. Officer Ryan pulled George over, and this time he was angry: "Aren't you the bloke I gave a warning to the other day?" George couldn't deny it. "Obviously you didn't learn your lesson. This time you won't get off so easy. You're booked. You'll have to appear in court to pay your fine, or you'll go to jail." George didn't thank him this time, but he didn't talk back either. How could he face Lucy? She'd be mad as hell. And of course she was. George tried to appease her. One night when she worked late, George met her at the door, naked, holding a freshly-baked lemon meringue pie. How could she stay mad?

On May 7, 1930, George appeared at the Criminal Courts Building on Franklin Street in lower Manhattan. "Be contrite," said Lucy, "and maybe you'll get off." But instead of being contrite or apologetic, George seemed slightly amused. "Twenty-five dollars or two nights in jail," said the judge, after hearing his case.

"Twenty-five plunkers for going just five miles over the speed limit?"

"Okay, forty dollars or three nights in jail," replied the judge. "Case closed." This time George kept his mouth shut.

So three nights in jail it was. Lucy cried bitterly as they handcuffed her husband like a common criminal and led him across the walkway to the Manhattan House of Detention, otherwise known as "The Tombs." There for three nights he shared a cell with another inmate, and later remembered those as the worst nights of his life.

In late May, when it was time for renewal, his license was refused. So he and Lucy sold the car to friends for $25. It had been an expensive adventure. They moved to a two-room apartment with a kitchenette and a tiny bath at 364 West 11th Street, back in their beloved Village, and could easily walk to the book shop from there. Amazingly, as a result of this incident, George had no criminal record. So there it is, the true story of the incident that clouded my childhood.

Early in 1931 George somehow obtained contraband copies of James Joyce's *Ulysses*. Although it had been published in Paris by Sylvia Beach in 1922, *Ulysses* was considered pornographic in the United States, and having it in your possession, much less selling it, was illegal. Government agents (F.B.I.?) confronted George at the book shop, demanding the remaining copies of *Ulysses* and the names of customers to whom he'd sold the book. At first he refused, and was cited for disobeying the law and threatened with an arrest. Then he turned over the copies, but said—probably truthfully—that he had no record of the customers who had bought it. And he refused to tell the agents how he had obtained the stock. For this he paid a $50 fine, and received a stiff warning, but that was all. In the U.S. sale of *Ulysses* became legal in 1933, eleven years after its original publication.

PART TWO

HARD TIMES

"At 7:15 the party began. It took about an hour, and I seemed to have yelled plenty."

Three Pregnancies and Two Births

So there they were, George and Lucy, after their first four years of marriage. Despite the lost ring, the robbery, the jail time, the quarrels, the moves; despite his recalcitrance and unwillingness to be "tamed," and despite her high expectations and disappointments, in fact despite their disappointments in each other, Lucy looked back on these early years as "lovely, happy-go-lucky times." The spring of 1931 would bring new challenges.

First there was Sigismund. During my childhood, in addition to my parents, sister, and me, there was an added presence in our household: Sigismund. When the dumbwaiter or refrigerator door was left gaping, a spill appeared on the carpet, or an unseemly spot on the blue chair, one of my parents would say, "Must be Sigismund." Sigismund was the unseen, unheard, mischief-maker in our lives. "Who is Sigismund?" I often asked my parents, but never received a satisfactory answer. "Oh, he's just a presence," or "He's a gremlin," or "He's just make-believe," they'd say. Nothing more.

I felt neither fear nor jealousy towards Sigismund: on the contrary, he was a benevolent presence on whom I was happy to deflect blame. Kitty and I simply accepted this being as part of our household. "Can Sigismund come to Jones Beach with us?" No, Sigismund always had to stay at home. This made me sad. He caused problems, yes, but since he also took the blame, I was very fond of him.

Sigismund first became a reality in 1931, a very uneven year for Lucy and George. They alternated between bitter quarrels and sweet lovemaking. The combination of a confrontational woman and a passive man—especially when the woman was also demanding and the man irresponsible—made for difficult times. But they had a mutual goal: despite their poverty, they planned a trip to London that summer. It would be a bookseller's dream to search its renowned antiquarian book shops for fine editions of George's favorites: Dickens, Trollope, Swinburne, Yeats, Marlowe, and of course anything pertaining to Shakespeare.

How could they afford this trip? First, in early January, they moved to a small, rear apartment at 19 West 8th Street, overlooking a dingy courtyard criss-crossed with clothes lines. Since the rent was only $50, Lucy insisted they put aside the ten dollars saved monthly. They played gin rummy together several nights a week, with the loser adding his losses to the trip piggy bank. And Lucy insisted on further austerity measures. But then, as always, any pressure on George backfired. Lucy wrote in February: "I am furious with GK for not telling me things. He gets worse and worse. We had our worst quarrel. I accuse him of lying. He drinks heavily. I throw the balance of wine into the sink, and also the gin. He is furious with me. He is impossible to live with." But the next month when George gave her a garnet ring for her thirty-third birthday, Lucy wrote that she was "so in love again." Once again George paid for the ring in installments.

And in May after another quarrel, Lucy wrote: "Oh dear, I think this is *the* fateful day! I'm indignant because he doesn't tell me things; he's peeved because I rage." And then for a week George neither bathed nor shaved, got to work on time or to bed on time. Lucy added: "Tonight he evades me when I ask him where he eats. I'll close my thoughts and actions just as tightly as he does. If it wears out our marriage it's okay by me. I won't have a 'don't care, no effort, close-mouthed' husband." And soon thereafter she wrote: "Oh, how I love that boy!"

Amidst the quarrels and lovemaking, their social life remained undiminished. They continued to eat at the Jumble Shop, Napoleon's, and sometimes at Child's, which offered "all you can eat" for sixty-cents. They entertained frequently and often George brought friends home for all-night games of chess or checkers. Bill and Florence Griffith offered them a two-week stay at their cottage on Swan Island, Maine (a thirty minute boat ride from Mt. Desert Island), where Lucy's mother Ada and grandmother Kitty joined them "for a blissful period of loafing, a glorious time."

George and Lucy at Swan Island, Maine, Summer, 1931.

All too soon that glorious time ended. Lucy, feeling nauseated, consulted a doctor and was diagnosed as being seven weeks' pregnant. Since neither Lucy nor George believed this diagnosis, they went to Napoleon's for dinner where, Lucy wrote: "George was hilarious. I love him so." But soon a second opinion confirmed the first. How could they have been so careless? Pregnancy presented a huge problem. A baby would end their carefree days, probably force them to close the book shop and find more lucrative work; damage, if not ruin, their marriage. They named the fetus Sigismund. What to do about Sigismund?

They decided to end the pregnancy as quickly as possible. But how? Abortions were illegal and, when performed as "back street affairs," all too frequently ended up with the death of the mother. At that time, fifteen hundred women a year died in New York City from infection or hemorrhaging after abortions. No doctor could openly perform one and expect to keep his license, but Lucy and George found Dr. Washak, who agreed to perform an undercover abortion. Since everything had to be done in secret, they promised to inform neither family nor friends.

On the evening of July 22, 1931, with Lucy nine weeks pregnant, they took a taxi to Dr. Washak's office. She wrote: "At 7:15 the party began. It took about an hour, and I seemed to have yelled plenty." They held hands during the taxi ride home and, according to Lucy, "George was *very* sweet and *very* relieved." And how was Lucy? She doesn't say. The abortion and two follow-up visits cost $75, which they paid in five monthly installments.

Lucy, anemic because of blood loss, was unable to climb the four flights to their apartment, so Margaret Freeman generously lent them her garden apartment at 111 Waverly Place, which had an elevator. George was happy to cook Lucy plenty of red meat, and to make her eggnogs daily. While recovering, Lucy enjoyed the radio in Margaret's apartment, and listened to *Lum and Abner*, *The Ed Sullivan Show*, and Kate Smith. And Lucy caught up on her reading: *The Good Earth*, *Sanctuary*, and dipped into the new cookbook, *The Joy of Cooking*. Their first walk was up Fifth Avenue to 34th to see the Empire State Building, the just-opened tallest skyscraper in the world.

By mid-August life was back to normal, except for one thing: Dr. Washak had discovered a growth on Lucy's right side the size of an orange. As she felt no pain, they decided to do nothing. Life went on much as before Sigismund, with continued socializing, entertaining, drinking, and long walks. One Sunday they walked up to 168th Street. There they stopped for iced drinks, and then crossed to New Jersey on the mile-long newly constructed George Washington Bridge. They walked back across, and then took a subway home. Their savings were demolished, they were once again in debt, all hopes of a London trip were dashed, but it was worth it. They never once regretted their decision. "So much in love it is grand!" wrote Lucy.

This, then, according to Lucy's diary is the true story of Sigismund. At ninety, Mother told me that the abortion was the most terrible experience of her life. She almost died. "I could never have gone through with it again," she said.

They moved once again, this time to a studio apartment at 216 Thompson Street, and borrowed money from Eddie Bierstadt to purchase Christmas and Hanukah cards. In late August Lucy visited Cleveland, where she solicited card orders from friends and family. Back in New York she looked for work, but refused an offer by publisher George Hecht as assistant editor of *School Management* because the salary was too low. George was glad about this: he wanted her at the book shop because she drew in customers. In truth, she wanted to be there too. They were "getting along swell."

In September 1931 the shop to the east of them became vacant, and George and Lucy decided to enlarge their space. Don't ask me how they managed this financially, but they did. Once again George painted and built new shelving, and by November business was good in their expanded shop. Lucy's mother and brother Bill visited at Christmastime. They all went to see Katherine Cornell portray Elizabeth Barrett in the new play, *The Barretts of Wimple Street.*

But all was not well. The tumor began to give Lucy trouble. She often felt sick, and by February it was so large that she felt she would need to have it removed. Also, because of the abortion and the tumor, her menstrual periods remained irregular. One day in March, after several months' absence, their old customer Dr. Fralick ("the cadger") returned to the shop. Lucy came around from behind the counter to give him a hug. After kissing her cheek, he looked down: "Well, well, when's the baby due?"

"Oh, I'm not pregnant. I have a tumor but it's not dangerous. It's a fibroid."

"Well, you're going to drop that fibroid on the floor in about two months," replied the doctor.

And that, dear reader, believe it or not, is the story of how Lucy first realized she might be pregnant with Kitty.

Lucy visited Dr. Shields and learned that the tumor had shrunk, and that indeed she was seven months' pregnant. Unbelievable! She took George to dinner at the Jumble Shop, and after a drink or two, told him the news. What to do? It was too late for an abortion. Within a couple of months, totally unprepared for a child, they were to become parents. The news spread quickly; they were the butt of many jokes, and Lucy was dubbed "The Madonna of 8th Street." For a time in April 1932 the world was riveted by a horrendous crime: the kidnapping and subsequent murder of the twenty-month-old Lindbergh baby. Sorrow over that infant's death made Lucy and George feel more loving towards the baby they would soon have.

Baby Kitty was born on May 26, 1932. Here's what Lucy wrote about the birth: "We had not seen the Bierstadts for a few weeks when their maid came into the shop. I asked, 'How are the Bierstadts?' She rolled her eyes and said: 'Oh Mr.

Bierstadt, he dead!' At that I had my first labor pains. The pains kept coming all night. GK got me to Booth Memorial Hospital about 9:00 the next morning, and Kitty was delivered by Dr. Shields about 5:00 p.m." The baby was named Catherine Ada Kirk after Lucy's beloved grandmother and mother.

Lucy and George with baby Kitty, 1932.

Surprisingly, Lucy loved having a baby. She wheeled Kitty down 8th Street in her buggy, calling out and waving to all she met: "Look what I've got!" Friends were more than generous: at one time Kitty had 101 dresses. That summer the new family visited friends in New Jersey, Connecticut, Pennsylvania, Woodstock, New York, and Cape Cod. According to Lucy, "It was a great life."

Proud and happy with Kitty as they were, they had not the space, the time, nor the money to care for her. And so by great good luck for all concerned, in September 1932 Lucy's mother Ada gladly brought four-month-old Kitty back to Cleveland, where she and her husband Joe gave their first grandchild full and loving attention. This separation was very, very hard for Lucy. How was it for George? She doesn't say.

Lucy insisted they make every effort to bring baby Kitty back. First they needed more space, so in January 1933 they moved to 45 Charles Street, a floor-through apartment (meaning that it had windows facing the front and the back) large enough to accommodate the baby. They bought a desk for $25, a cedar chest for the baby's clothes, and a much-needed mattress. And then they needed more money. George tried for a moonlighting position at $30 a week, but this did not materialize. They borrowed money from friends; $80 here, and $100 there, and in mid-February Lucy fetched eight-month-old Kitty from Cleveland.

Four generations—
baby Kitty,
Grandma Ada,
Great-Grandma Kitty,
Lucy
July, 1932.

Problems piled up. In May George received a summons for $215 back rent. Fortunately, this case was settled out of court for only $50. That same month Lucy missed her period. Maybe the new mattress was a bad idea. A visit to Dr. Shields confirmed their worst suspicions; Lucy was indeed pregnant again. Although she took six castor oil tablets and hot baths daily trying, if possible, to abort, nothing worked.

"How did you feel when you found you were pregnant again?" I asked Mother, after hearing about the abortion and about Kitty's birth. "Oh just fine. Actually happy. We thought, well, we already have one. We might as well have another. And I'm so glad we did! What would I ever have done without you?"

Still I had my doubts and reading her diary after her death confirmed my suspicions. They *really* had not wanted any children. And I can understand. It was the depth of the Depression, a terrible time to bring children into the world. When Roosevelt took office in February 1933 unemployment was at 37%: fourteen million Americans were out of work. It's no wonder that the book shop was struggling too.

All in all, the summer of 1933 was miserable. George cut his hand badly on a chisel, needed many stitches, and was unable to work. In July they spent a week in New Canaan with the Manns, hoping for a break from the unbearable heat, but there it was 114 in the shade. Lucy was nauseous. To make things worse, Scottie, anxious to have a baby herself, was envious rather than supportive of her friend. There was one bright spot in New Caanan: Scottie and Bob had a radio, and they listened one Sunday evening to Roosevelt's Fireside Chat. Once back in the Village George resumed his old habits staying out late night after night with neither explanation nor apology. "The straws are piling high..." wrote Lucy.

They needed more money. Lucy toyed with the idea of getting a real estate certificate. She offered to review books for the *Greenwich Villager*. She tried selling holiday cards to department stores. No takers. They had to face facts: they simply couldn't afford to care for a baby. And so once again in late October Lucy's mother came to the rescue. After visiting for a week, she took Kitty back to Cleveland. Lucy cried and cried. She determined to ensure that the holiday season was lucrative, and then bring Kitty back. But first, there was another baby to be born. Here, in Mother's words, is the story of my birth:

> The Friday before Mary's birth (three days before), after straightening the shop and getting the stock out for the next day, Myron Parrott came over to our apartment at 3:00 a.m. and we drank rum tea all night. Myron told us how his wife, Lucille, died of a mysterious ailment after the birth of her second child and of the staggering expenses incurred by her special care. The next day GK and I crawled home at 11:00 so weary and dejected. But then we had to pep up for Willie and Myrtle O'Neil who made a special trip to celebrate. Bill brought a lovely bottle of whiskey, which went well with appetizers GK prepared. They left at 3:00 a.m. GK and I crept into bed, anticipating the first eight hour sleep in weeks.

On Sunday, Christmas Eve 1933, I cooked an excellent breakfast, and GK and I prepared in a leisurely manner to go to the book shop for last minute customers. GK left at 4:00 p.m. and I went walking and shopping for a few little Christmas gifts. At 6:00 I went to the book shop, but there was no business. Mary Tobin arrived and we partied on the O'Neil offering. At 8:00 we went to Napoleon's for an excellent meal with cocktails and wine.

Home at midnight after buying flowers and groceries for Christmas breakfast, to which we had invited Mary Tobin and John Holman. To bed at 1:00 a.m., tired, elated, feeling fine. After an hour a pain, followed in rhythmic succession by more. With difficulty I roused the slumbering GK who phoned Dr. Shields at 3:00 a.m. She advised the hospital at once, though I explained I had had something to drink. At 4:00 a.m. we arrived at the hospital, by 5:00 Lu was all ready for the delivery room and trundled upstairs past a pale GK who admonished, 'Be brave.'

Mary Daler Kirk, 5# 13 oz., expected January 9 or later in 1934 arrived at 6:55 a.m. on Monday, Christmas morning. It seems Lu had a *much easier time than with Kitty*. No forceps were needed. At 7:00 a.m. Lu was in a four bed ward having produced little Mary, just as carolers in the park across sang 'Noel, Noel, Noel, Noel, born is the king of Israel.' Lu heard Dr. Shields say: 'Oh, it's a little girl; she wanted a boy.' I thought Dr. Shields did not get to the hospital in time to deliver the baby, and said to her, 'Oh, you just took care of the afterbirth.' Dr. Shields was furious with me.

George came in for a few minutes, and then went home to breakfast and to phone Cleveland, the O'Neil's, and many other friends. Lu was crazy for sleep. I felt hurt and incensed that the baby came early, as I had counted on two weeks' sleep to make up for the terrific Christmas rush strain. Two hypos and two sleeping powders failed, and I was not to know sleep until late Christmas night.

What to call the new baby girl? Since Lucy named Kitty, it was George's turn to decide. He and Scottie suggested many names, settling on Mary Daler Kirk, after George's mother, Mary Elizabeth (Mellie) Daler Kirk.

Sixty years later, sitting there on Mother's gold couch, holding the hand of this dear, frail woman, I thought about the loss of Sigismund, who would have been our older brother; the loss of the trip to England; the loss of the bookshop several years later; the death of my father thirty years earlier, and was reminded of the many things Lucy thought would be, but never were. And of the many things she'd thought would never be, but were.

Lucy and Mary Daler Kirk. 1934.

A note from Alfred Goldsmith, bookseller, on Kitty's birth, 1932.

"I regret having life flow so aimlessly. We do so little every day—we get up late, drink too much, and now I might even be a widow soon."

First You Say You Do

The next period of George and Lucy's life was characterized by doubt and indecision. Would George leave Lucy? Would Lucy leave George? Could they keep the book shop? Could they raise the children? They even wondered whether the new baby would live. Lucy was incensed with the baby for arriving so early, and preventing her from attending Alice Hurtilsbe's New Year's Eve party, and incensed with George for going alone. Prohibition had ended just weeks before, and liquor would be flowing freely. And I was scarcely eating. For the first four weeks I drank only about half an ounce, when I was, according to Dr. Shields, supposed to drink three. George confessed to Lucy that he feared I would not live. And so did Lucy. But live I did, and soon began to thrive.

Lucy's first trip out of the house, in late January 1934, was to get fitted for a new diaphragm, as George was becoming so amorous: "Poor George feels I don't give him enough sex life unless I'm a willing partner at least once a day. I'd be one—gladly—if I could ever be un-tired and un-sleepy enough," she wrote.

But she had other things on her mind too. Now that they had two little girls, she was determined to raise and educate us well. George, however, remained his old self; careless about money, drinking excessively, and refusing to explain or justify his long absences. On their seventh anniversary in March, instead of coming home early as promised, he arrived at 2:00 a.m., saying he "met a chap and played checkers." Lucy spent the evening reading Steinbeck's new novel, *Tortilla Flat*.

Two weeks later Lucy brought me at three months to her parents' house in Cleveland. Kitty, at twenty-two months, did not recognize her, which broke her heart. Lucy took a job at Higbee's department store. I believe she seriously considered leaving George at that time, but a month later, in mid-April, she returned to New York with Kitty and me in tow. For her thirty-sixth birthday George gave her a bottle of sherry: "I *never* want liquor for a present! He knows that!" she wrote in her diary.

One night in May, coming home late and drunk, George told Lucy some harsh truths: "He confessed that he could never love me as he once did because I had done some 'deceitful things,'—that one night he determined not to come home again, planned to skip the state. Thought it over, and decided it wasn't worth it. If I were half-way decent to him he'd stick it out. He likes the kids, but they sometimes get on his nerves. While I was away he had designs on some girl—a literary customer—who did not respond and treated him like a shop-keeper. Then he went into a coma and I did all the dishes, rinsed diapers, got

Ada and Joseph Dvorak, the Cleveland grandparents, 1930s.

him to bed at 4:30. I would not be surprised to be a deserted wife." And yet she stayed. And so did he.

That summer George's friend Howard Lovecraft visited, and those two spent several evenings together, talking and walking—once from Brooklyn Heights to Greenwich Village. And we too had long outings, when the weather was nice and our parents had free time—to Battery Park or to Central Park Zoo. Kitty and I were thriving, much too young to know about or care about our parents' troubles. At a check-up for us, Dr. Shields said: "You two have the nicest babies I've ever seen: both small and good gainers." But Lucy voiced a serious concern: Kitty's fontanel had not fully closed, and

Kitty and George at the piers, New York City, 1934.

she feared the baby would be an idiot. Dr. Shields, looking directly at Lucy, replied: "If there's an idiot in the family, it's *not* the baby!" Much to Lucy's delight, George said that night: "I love you for giving me such nice children, and no matter how ornery they may turn out, I'll still love them."

The summer brought more problems. First, Lucy found bedbugs in the apartment. Then a boy playing ball fell on me in the carriage and—although I screamed and screamed—I was only slightly bruised. To top it all off, Lucy found a suspicious note in George's pocket: "Tonight?" Was it innocuous? She never knew, and neither do we, but she wrote: "He never knows when to say 'no' or when to stop drinking. I feel like leaving him for good, as he's turned most insensitive and ungrateful." That night, however, Lucy made sure they spent together: they went to the new musical, *Anything Goes*, and came home humming songs from it: "I Get a Kick out of You" and "You're the Top."

In August, after two weeks' respite with Scottie and Bob in Connecticut, they came home to further troubles. A sheriff served George with a summons for payment of $240 overdue back rent, and the property owner raised the monthly rent from $125 to $140. What to do? They begged and borrowed money for the back rent. Lucy, feeling rocky, drinking too much, and worried about another pregnancy, consulted her doctor. Dr. Shields assured her she was not pregnant, but in a state of nervous exhaustion, and administered a sedative. Something had to be done. In September 1934 grandma Ada once again eased the situation, and brought Kitty and me back to Cleveland. Later that month they saw Gershwin's wonderful musical: *Porgy and Bess* and the new movie from Dashiell Hammett's book, *The Thin Man*.

"I *must* find work so we can care for the children in New York," Lucy wrote. She did her very best. She took a temporary job at *Campfires* for $25 a week. She promoted the book shop on radio station WOR. She spoke to NYU Wives about holiday books available at the shop. And her efforts paid off. On December 22 she wrote: "A $200 day! We are so tired and so pleased. Working day and night for the past two weeks, with Myron (Parrott) and Harvey working right with us."

Lucy hoped for a quiet, romantic New Year's Eve, but instead George brought Harvey home for dinner and a night of chess. She spent the evening reading the new bestseller, *Tender Is the Night*. Lucy liked Harvey, but felt he never knew when to leave.

1934 was a year not just of family problems, of course. It was also a year of violent crimes, and of the death of several notorious criminals, all shot down by the police: John Dillinger, Pretty Boy Floyd, and Bonnie and Clyde. Although they each saw themselves as robinhood figures, robbing from the rich and supposedly giving to the needy—and were romanticized by the public as such—they left a wake of innocent victims in their paths. Compared to their crimes, my parents' troubles seem minor.

One night in January 1935 George wanted a beer at work, but Lucy was adamant: "*No! No drinking on the job!*" Then she found an empty bottle of Applejack in his pocket. George threatened to leave for good. She threw a bottle of ink into the fireplace. She expressed her concern about his alcohol consumption, and insisted he see his doctor. Bill Birnkrant, the doctor, gave him some serious news: one more year of heavy drinking would finish him. Lucy wrote: "I regret having life flow so aimlessly. We do so little every day—we get up late, drink too much, and now I might even be a widow soon." But nothing seems to have changed much.

Lucy wanted her children back, yes, but not under these circumstances. So when her mother phoned in late February saying she was exhausted and bringing us back to New York, Lucy wrote: "Life seems wretched." When George and Lucy met us at Grand Central—Kitty (almost three) I (barely a year) and Grandma (fifty-nine)—we were all sick. Grandma Ada was immediately hospitalized with pneumonia and then—rather than staying with us—she took a hotel room for three weeks before returning to Cleveland. Lucy wrote: "There is *so much work* with two babes—constant meals, baths, etc." The care of us intensified the tension between them, and one night Lucy pummeled George and left him with a black eye. "Goodie," she wrote. And in March: "My thirty-seventh birthday, and a busy but unromantic one it is."

They needed help badly, and hired a woman named Gussie to do childcare and to help around the apartment. This freed Lucy up to spend more time at the shop, which George and Harvey were painting and remodeling, hoping to improve business. She wrote: "George is a whiz at it. God, I love him. Poor, ambitious lad, I'm so proud of him." Their efforts paid off, and Easter was a busy, profitable season.

After letting Gussie go, we all spent July with Hedwig and Bob Spears in Middleton, New York. Although Lucy vowed she would abstain from alcohol this month, Bob was a heavy drinker, and George was happy to join him. Hedwig and Bob had a new game, Monopoly, which the adults enjoyed playing. And they had a radio and enjoyed listening to *Fibber McGee and Molly*. I was teething and fussy. On our return to the Village, Lucy accepted a part-time job for $50 a month as associate editor of *School Management*. This enabled our family to move to a larger apartment at 32 King Street which, according to Lucy, was "our best apartment yet: so roomy, spacious, with windows facing both front and back, plenty of closets, nice sink and a nice yard." George built us a sandbox, which we loved.

For a while life was better, with Lucy's new job and the new apartment. They hired Margaret Czernieski to care for Kitty and me. In September 1935, little Kitty barely three-years-old started pre-school at the Little Red Schoolhouse. The Little Red Schoolhouse, founded in 1921 by Elizabeth Irwin, was New York City's first progressive school—based on the principles of John Dewey to promote independent thinkers, creativity, and lifelong learners. I stayed home with Margaret who, according to Lucy, was "excellent, very conscientious, five star."

Kitty's teacher donated a turkey to our family for Thanksgiving, and joined us at dinner, along with many other guests. Lucy, now happy with George, delighted him with *The Oxford Shakespeare* for his thirty-seventh birthday. He and Harvey, having completed the remodeling of the book shop, were "gay and festive," certain their efforts would pay off and allow George to pay the three months' back rent due. And although the shop had a successful holiday season, on Christmas Eve Lucy wrote: "I know GK ain't bought me nothing. Too busy."

We spent Christmas day at home, my second birthday. Many guests came bearing many gifts, and some stayed until 4:00 a.m. Lucy wrote: "Kids were so sweet, dear, and lovely. I'm so glad they were here with us this year." New Year's Eve George and Lucy stayed home alone, but on New Year's Day thirty friends came over for rum punch.

At the beginning of 1936, thanks to Roosevelt's Civilian Conservation Corps (CCC) and the Works Projects Administration (WPA), unemployment was down to 17%. But it was still the heart of the Depression. Even with Lucy's job, we were living below the poverty line, which was set at $1300 for a family of four. Very few had extra money to buy books, the shop was bringing in almost nothing, and George had just signed a two year lease at $140 a month.

In January 1936, at barely two, I also started pre-school at the Little Red Schoolhouse. Lucy wrote: "Their teacher, Miss Carter, is crazy about them. Mary tries to talk. She is so lovely. Her cheeks are brilliant red these days." That month, during a bitter cold spell, the apartment's pipes froze and the gas had to be turned off. We huddled under heavy blankets, but still Kitty and I both developed earaches and deep coughs. On our recovery, however, we were out in our wonderful yard happily making a snowman. Temporarily, at least, life seemed good.

George and Lucy hoped that Valentine's cards at the shop would bring in $400, but they nowhere near achieved that goal. Then George pinned high hopes on a new catalog, but Lucy remained doubtful, and her doubts proved valid. There was no business, and the shop's bank account was depleted. "But *still*," wrote Lucy, "GK *loves* buying books for the CBS, even though God knows we can't afford them!"

In March George and Lucy celebrated their ninth anniversary and Lucy's thirty-eighth birthday. George pleased her with violets and a pair of "lovely Jensen earrings." But the best present of all was George's decision to "go on the wagon," and for several weeks he had neither liquor nor cigarettes. They worked hard and played hard, often getting to bed at 4:00 a.m., and they were getting along swell, completely unaware of what troubles would descend on them soon.

Mary and Kitty at their grandparents' home in Cleveland, summer 1935. Photographer unknown.

"Terrible to hand two blanket-swathed babes to hospital orderly. He carries them to the ambulance through a gaping crowd....I can scarcely contain my tears. I'm so worried and so weary."

Babes in Arms

1936 was a terrible, turbulent time in the western world, and troubles in our family were only a microcosm of what was happening elsewhere. Stalin began his purges, Trotsky was exiled, Japan invaded China, the Spanish Civil War began, and Germany re-occupied the Rhineland. In the United States, one very good thing happened: the Social Security program was enacted. Here's what was happening in our household.

On May 1, 1936, shortly before her 4th birthday, Kitty developed a high fever. Although Lucy feared the worst—Scarlet Fever, which was raging in the city—thank goodness *that* was not the case. But it was the beginning of something even worse; our serious childhood illnesses, which lasted for close to three months. I turn directly to Lucy's diary for her detailed account of this time.

> May 3. Kitty's sickness diagnosed as measles. Dr. Bill Birnkrant, who's attending Kitty, says to keep Mary away from her; maybe she won't catch the measles. Mary is such a lamb. I order her to stay out of middle room where Kitty's been moved. She obeys sweetly—just coming to the door, but not crossing the threshold. I say 'Don't come in, dear.' She replies, 'Momma, I wo.' Kitty is a very sick little girl, so GK takes care of a darling Mary. Takes her riding. She sings and dances and they have a wonderful time together.
>
> May 6. Mary breaks out too...so she goes to bed. We don't think she'll be as sick as Kitty, as she is very gay.
>
> May 11. Oh what a day! Kitty and Mary's ears ache. Bill (Birnkrant) says they are both very sick: will have pneumonia within twenty-four hours. We get Miss Josie Shields,

a nurse, for the night. George, Margaret (our caregiver), Bill and I are in tears. Kitty's lips are cracked: gangrene may set in!!! Bill orders a bromide for me. George and I go to bed about 1:00, leaving capable Josie in charge.

May 12. Oh how sick is Mary! Josie takes her in front room, puts her head on a pillow, gives her a 'liquid diet.' Mary so low at noon, fever 106. Bill advises Willard Parker Hospital for Contagious Diseases. He phones the Health Department, as they have to send a doctor to pass on the case. It's noon—they promise a doctor in two hours. Mary steadily worse. Turns blue in the face. Still no doctor. (Our friend) Mary Tobin stays with us all day. She and Bill keep on calling the Health Department. Poor Mary is very, very sick. Fights sleeping on a pillow, and raises her temperature more! Mary Tobin phones Judge Bertha Schwartz, who phones the Mayor's office.

It was ghastly waiting all day while babes got worse. Bill and Mary stayed by. George was in the book shop and we kept him posted by phone on the state of the babes. At 7:00 p.m. a doctor arrived, and immediately admitted both kids to the hospital. It was about 8:00 when the ambulance arrived. A nice nurse, Miss Witmer, on her first week of ambulance service, and a dumb but nice porter, Raymond, in attendance. Miss W. says, 'Just undress the babes, put on these hospital pajamas, and wrap them up in these woolen blankets.' Miss W. and I do it, while our sick babes protest. Finally accomplished, Miss W. takes information, and I hand each darling form to Raymond. Terrible to hand two blanket-swathed babes to hospital orderly. He carries them to the ambulance through a gaping crowd. I couldn't even ride in the ambulance as babes were 'contagious.' Such comments:

'Ooh look!'

'Is she dead?'

'Oh, she's turned yellow!'

'Here's another one!'

'Is she dead?'

'No, she's turned yellow too.'

'It's the babies.'

'Ooh!'

'I wonder who's coming out next.'

Mary Tobin and I drove to the hospital with Bill. Many friends offered us money. We accepted $300, as we were penniless.

Thursday, May 14. Visit hospital, as both kids are on 'critical' list. Kitty awake and very tearful. Mary breathing heavily, still bluish, with a big sign on her bed: 'Very Special Precautions.' She was the only one in the ward with such a card! Each babe is in a 3-sided glass cubicle—open to the front—middle of the room. Parents stay outside the glass, covered with sterile smock. It's highly unsatisfactory, and I resolve not to go back till babes are discharged. Luckily, they did not have to give Mary oxygen.

Saturday, May 16. Hospital tells us they are 'out of danger.'

Sunday, May 17. Lu goes to visit and is overwhelmed to learn both babes are being discharged! What a mess! All our blankets are at the cleaners, Margaret has gone home (as Bill thought kids would spend three weeks in hospital)—well, I madly got GK on the phone, and he and I collected our dearly beloveds. The shock was almost too much for us. Reason for discharge? They *were* over measles, but still had badly runny ears, which had 'broken naturally' on May 14. Hospital was crowded, and scarlet fever also raged. So we were advised home was best. Mary Tobin, Martha, Judy, arrived bringing heavy blankets, and we put our dear supine babes to bed. GK so relieved! He said he couldn't tell anyone how sick they had been. Thank goodness for the bromides. Otherwise I wouldn't have been able to stand it. The babes slept well Sunday night too.

May 18-21 (Monday through Thursday). Babes in bed, still with fever, but nice and good children, with runny ears. It is so *swell* to have them home! Thursday Lu had to go to the office. Josie, the good nurse, came in for the day.

Friday, May 22. Bill called early: prescribed *dry cotton plugs* every hour for draining ears, much food, open bowels. Mary coughs too much. As her eyes itch, he prescribes boric acid solution. Josie delicately brought up question of Bill's treatment of babes, being of the rather lackadaisical 'let's see what happens' variety, which it undoubtedly is! So I ask him about a consultant on the ears. We both agree on the best in the city, Dr. Fowler, the director of the Eye, Ear, Nose, and Throat Hospital. So I phone him.

Saturday, May 23. Margaret and I take Kitty and Mary, bundled well, in a taxi to Dr. Fowler. He says: 'Oh, I can see they have been *very* sick little girls!' Prescribes three ear irrigations a day for each. They both have mastoiditis, aggravated by large tonsils and adenoids. Our Kitty may need an operation. Oh, that awful first irrigation! Lu tries to give it to Kitty in her bed. Wets mattress, wall, Kitty, Margaret, and self! Puts Mary in Kitty's bed. Not much better! The poor kids. They shriek while Margaret and I doggedly continue.

May 24. Miss Brown, a practical nurse, comes to help. She's very good. She puts kids on sink board and lays the bag for bath under, puts rubber sheet around them, and then it works much better. Mary, after a few days, gets to like it. Each ear gets three irrigations a day: one quart *hot* sterile water with one tablespoon salt added.

May 25. I take Kitty to Dr. Fowler, and Mary stays in bed. Mary eats very well and, except for her fever, performs very well. Not so our Kitty. Dr. thinks Kitty needs an operation *at once*!

June 1. Kitty is rushed to Manhattan Eye, Ear, Nose and Throat Hospital. At 4:00 her left ear is operated on. I died many deaths before Dr. Fowler came out at 5:45. Operation a success, but he would make no further comment.

June 4. Mary, normal for nearly two weeks, runs a temperature of 101.4 and has a rash. Take her to Dr. Fowler, who says to irrigate every three hours and to bring her to the clinic tomorrow. She is gay, sprightly, and talks nice long sentences. None is plain.

FORM 7 5M 3-35 · EAR CLINIC

MANHATTAN EYE, EAR and THROAT HOSPITAL
210 EAST 64TH STREET, BETWEEN 2ND AND 3RD AVES., NEW YORK
COME TUESDAYS, THURSDAYS, and SATURDAYS at 2 P.M.

SURGEON-DIRECTOR, DR. EDMUND P. FOWLER
SURGEON, DR. L. M. HUBBY
JUNIOR SURGEON, DR. C. W. DEPPING
ASSISTANT SURGEONS

| Dr. J. C. Sharp | Dr. I. I. Alper | Dr. E. P. Fowler, Jr. |
| Dr. J. R. Emery | Dr. E. E. Harrison | Dr. A. A. Cirillo |

CLINICAL ASSISTANTS
Dr. R. C. Seeley
Dr. M. Stein

DR. FOWLER

Mary Kirk

No. 155853   JUN 2 - 1936   Age 2

NONE TREATED EXCEPT THOSE WHO ARE TOO POOR TO PAY FOR MEDICAL ADVICE

ALWAYS BRING THIS CARD WITH YOU

June 6. Mary not so well, feverish. Swollen neck and ear. There's quite a lump under her right ear. Dr. Fowler says: 'Take her to the hospital. We'll keep her under observation for a few days.' I can scarcely contain my tears. I'm so worried and so weary. Lu took her right to the hospital in a taxi. Mary cried all the way there, and wept bitterly when Dr. Fowler examined her. Called GK who rushed up with her measles certificate and we put her in a little bed in the ward just beside our darling, sleeping Kitty, who had a huge bandage round her head. Mary has acute mastoiditis. Dr. Fowler does all he can to prevent an operation, and lo and behold, by constant X-rays, sulfa, and ice bags, he prevents it. But she is not discharged from the hospital for another month.

June 7. Visiting day. George tired and cross, so I go alone. Mary quite tearful as I leave. Kitty, head bandaged hugely, is lovely and understands. Mary weeps bitterly.

June 14. I visit with George and Bill. Mary, in a nightie with ice bag on her neck, weeps copiously and looks disgustedly at her apparel, in a much 'I don't yike' frame of mind.

June 16. Kitty's better. Mary's chipper. Lu registers at the Murray Hill Hotel for the night to get some sleep.

June 20. Ada and (brother) Bill arrive from Cleveland.

When we all visited Mary wept nearly all the time and is much ashamed of the ice bag around her neck and her nightie. Kitty had on pink pajamas.

June 29. George and Ada brought Kitty home from the hospital.

July 5. Mary discharged from the hospital after weeks of observation and many x-rays. She looks lovely, eats well, and has no more discharge or swollen glands. Still weighs 30#.

Lucy returned by train to New York after spending three weeks in Cleveland for a much-needed respite. The next week Lucy, George, Grandma Ada, Margaret, and we girls went to the Delaware Water Gap to start our recuperation.

After Kitty's operation, Lucy and George were determined to find a country house to rent for the summer so we could recuperate in healthy, rural air. Lucy's friend Catherine Wilson knew of such a house at the Delaware Water Gap. (The Water Gap is formed where the Delaware River cuts a large ridge of the Appalachian Mountains, and forms the border between Pennsylvania and New Jersey. It is about eighty miles northwest of Manhattan, near Stroudsburg, Pennsylvania).

And so they rented this eight room stone house 'with terrible furnishings' from mid-July to early September 1936, for $70 a month. The house, built in the 1850s, had a pump and a wood stove, but no indoor plumbing. The property included a small building called the Creek Cottage where sometimes George and Lucy honeymooned. It was a great gift to the entire family, and we thrived during our time there, the first of several idyllic vacations in that house.

Our household consisted of Grandma Ada, George, Lucy, our caregiver Margaret, Kitty, and me. Neighbors who became friends included the Cgr and Banholtz families. Many visitors came up for weekends, including Lu Phettaplace, Catherine Wilson, Mary Tobin, Bertha Schwartz, and Margaret Freeman. Aunt Nancy, Uncle Cecil, and Uncle Bill with his bride Babe visited also.

Grandma Ada, Lucy, George, Mary, Kitty
Delaware Water Gap, 1936

There was nothing for Kitty and me to do but play. We swam everyday in a nearby pond, which was formed by a slanted concrete wall on one side. The pond had a muddy, weedy bottom where black water snakes lurked. Neither of us feared them. We were naked or nearly naked most of the time, and Kitty tanned while I burned. We both got poison ivy. We searched for small critters, especially salamanders, which fascinated us with their changing colors. We took long walks to the quarry and to the spring. Kitty's hair, shaved for her operation, grew back in.

Lucy, at *School Management*, had to spend most weekdays in New York, joining us on weekends. She took the train from Manhattan to Johnsonville, New York, twelve miles from our rented house. Sometimes George walked to meet her and together they walked back home. "One night," wrote Lucy, "walked fifteen miles up a mountain, over the crest, and down the Appalachian Trail. It was the *best* walk in the moonlight!" Here are some other entries from Momma's diary that summer:

"Mary and Kitty went to the pond every day and just loved it. Ada stayed with us until July 25th. Mary is crazy about her. Mary's siege left her with two things to overcome: foot-stamping and screaming. We try to bring it down to a minimum."

"Babes get nicely brown and husky. Mr. and Mrs. Louis Cgr became their friends. As did the cows, horses, chickens, dogs, cats, and ducks. Mary gets over all her fear of dogs, and pets avidly. She loves to run, walk, play in sand, and then come home for milk. She's a dear about keeping off the road and out of the poison ivy patch."

84

I remember the upstairs bedroom with neither curtains nor shades where Kitty and I slept. We were fascinated by a mysterious bright light which regularly swept the sky. Momma said it was a beacon which kept airplanes safe from the mountains. At night she read us fairy tales, especially those of Hans Christian Anderson. Although Kitty and I cried over "The Little Match Girl," we wanted to hear it again and again. And then, after Momma kissed us goodnight and turned out the light, we listened to the whippoorwills and watched the beacon,

Mary and Kitty at Delaware Water Gap, 1936

which kept us safe too. Mostly, I remember experiencing peace and well-being there, which I had seldom felt before.

We had some exciting times too. One night a fox chased the neighbor's cat up a tree. The fire department was called, and they helped her down. One day, after seeing honey running down a wall, Kitty discovered a beehive in the house. How we got rid of the hive and whether or not we ate the honey neither of us remembers. And one day Daddy beheaded a copperhead he encountered at the pump. He was so proud.

In early September (1936) we took the train back to Manhattan. Mother began fulltime work editing both *School Management*, and the Metropolitan Section of *Parents' Magazine.* Full-time work was necessary, as hospital bills were $1500, and George owed several hundred dollars in back rent for the shop. Although Kitty and I were better, we stayed home with Margaret that fall, as we still had trouble with our ears and throats. On October 17 we had our tonsils removed. Here's what Momma wrote:

Take Mary and Kitty to Manhattan Eye, Ear, Nose and
Throat for tonsillectomies. Mrs. Roe, in the receiving office,

takes babes from George and me, and they go to their rooms without a murmur. Their rooms are $15 each. They are given ether. Dr. Fowler, bless his kindly old heart, performs both operations. Mary at 1:45 and Kitty immediately after. Lu sees Dr. Fowler at 4:30 and he says operations went okay. The next day at noon we were so surprised to see them up and dressed. We took them home in a taxi, Mary in fine fettle, full of the dickens, teases us on our way home, tickles us. Kitty not so gay.

We put them to bed for a week, put cold compresses on their necks, give them soda water to drink, soups and other liquids, and by Tuesday (day three) they are back on a regular diet with no fever, no earache, no sore throats!! Dr. Fowler justified my worst fears. Said they had terrible throats: he really was scared of the operations, feared further ear trouble. But now they are doing well.

In late November we returned to pre-school at the Little Red Schoolhouse. Only after our parents were sure we were out of danger, did they resume their social life. They enjoyed Wilder's play *You Can't Take It with You* and loved the Rogers and Hart musical, *On Your Toes.* They also loved Chaplin's film, *Modern Times.* For the rest of the year, having denied themselves fun for several months, they played hard.

George and Lucy had high expectations for excellent book and card sales that Christmas and business was so good they hired (Aunt) Bunny Hutchins. But in Cleveland Lucy's beloved grandmother, Kitty Ackley was failing, and Momma insisted on giving Kitty and me a last chance to see our great-grandmother. So on Christmas Eve, we three took the Empire State there, leaving Daddy alone for Christmas. She left a book with Daddy she hoped he would read: *How to Win Friends and Influence People.* She brought the runaway best-seller, *Gone with the Wind,* to read on the train. Great-grandma Kitty, lying in bed in the home of Aunt Nancy and Uncle Cecil, scarcely moved or spoke. Momma made Kitty and me go up and kiss her, which frightened me. I turned three on Christmas day.

On our return to New York, Lucy was dismayed to find a note from Margaret which said simply: "I can't work for you anymore. You'll have to find someone else." She offered no explanation. What to do?

CATALOGUE
of

AMERICANA • ART AND ILLUSTRATED BOOKS •
BOOKS ABOUT BOOKS • FIRST EDITIONS •
BOOKS ON THE THEATRE, ETC., ETC.

◆

CATALOGUE NUMBER FIVE
1936

◆

Chelsea Book Shop
58 WEST 8th STREET, NEW YORK CITY
Telephone: SPring 7 - 1382

OPEN EVENINGS

"If things continue as they are, I will divorce him. It's been a bad five years. If there's another girl he can have her. I'll give him up with no regrets."

Bad to Woise

As George would say, much of the next period went from bad to woise, and not only for our family, but for the country and for the western world. Times were bad, as Franklin Roosevelt said in his eloquent 1937 inaugural speech: "I see one third of a nation ill-housed, ill-clad, ill-nourished." In Europe, the Nazis excluded Jews from trade and industry, and forced them to wear the yellow Star of David; and in Russia Stalin tried hundreds of citizens as spies, thus increasing his political purge.

At home, Lucy hired twenty-one year old Rosie Martinelli to care for Kitty and me. Rosie was lovesick and—as it turned out—married and pregnant, although she didn't reveal the latter information to us. Her husband was a butcher, and during their courtship had locked her in the freezer until she said yes. She left him after a quarrel, when he threatened to do the same again. A good Catholic, she tried (in vain) to convert us all.

At the shop George received an ultimatum from his landlord, Mr. St. John. Unless he paid up the back rent, the book shop's lease would no longer be valid: from then on it would be honored only on a month to month basis. And then George received another blow. On March 15th his beloved friend Howard Lovecraft died, at 46, of colon cancer. George felt the book shop would be more successful if Lucy were there, and he wanted her back, saying she had a personality everyone liked. Although Lucy called this "high praise from Caesar," and willingly helped out when she could, her job and children consumed her. From then on, the Chelsea Book Shop was *his* baby. She had two babes at home to care for.

Truth be told, Lucy loved her job at *Parents'*, and loved the idea of being a "professional woman." Working in downtown Manhattan (52 Vanderbilt Avenue) within a stone's throw of Grand Central Station, and mingling with professional people daily, raised Lucy's expectations considerably. She wrote: "I hope someday to reach my most likely niche in life. I grow a bit ambitious now—would like prestige for George and me, nice surroundings and education for the dear babes—music, piano, opera, theatre, and exquisite clothes." She began weekly massage and body toning treatments. Her favorite place for cocktails became the Waldorf Astoria. Life was swell. On her 39th birthday she was pleased with George: "A happy one. Silver pin, cocktails, flowers, movie, dinner. Bless his honey heart."

But this appreciation was short-lived. In April, after he was out all night, she wrote: "I hate, hate, hate his nonsense. We are so far apart and it's due to his making no effort towards family life, 50-50 propositions, or any of the simple, easy things a man could do, that I'd leave him in a flash if it weren't for the children. I may annoy him as much as he does me—but he could *tell* me about it. He's just silent. We *could* love each other again, but George won't lift a finger. I'm getting awfully fed up with some of GK's less endearing childish behavior. If things continue on as they are, I will divorce him. It's been a bad five years. If there's another girl he can have her. I'll give him up with no regrets."

And then of course they made up and took us to the Bronx Zoo for a wonderful day. When we returned, Rosie was in the throes of labor pains. Daddy rushed her to the hospital and phoned her estranged husband. That was the last we saw of Rosie.

On the evening of May 6, 1937, the Hindenburg, a dirigible with almost one hundred people aboard, crashed to the ground as it was landing in New Jersey. Thirty-six people were killed in the crash, and the survivors suffered severe burns and other injuries. It was the death of the dream of transatlantic airships, much to the dismay of the western world.

Momma hired Margaret (I'm not sure of her last name) to care for us. Kitty broke out in a rash which—although it looked frightening and needed immediate attention—turned out to be eczema, something she would be plagued with throughout her childhood. Momma took us to Woolworth's, where we tried on hats just for fun. A few days later Kitty's head started itching, and Momma found a bug in her hair, and then another, and still another. She checked my hair, and found

Lucy checking Mary's hair for lice, Delaware Water Gap, July, 1937.

bugs there too. Head lice. Momma and Margaret worked hard to get rid of them, and it was a nasty process: rubbing turpentine into our scalps until they burned. This treatment eventually did the trick, but not until we had infected many of our classmates.

Summer came, and with it temporary respite. In June once again our parents rented the Delaware Water Gap house, this time for three months. Kitty had just turned five and I was three and a half. Sometimes Daddy was there with us, sometimes Momma, sometimes both, but Daddy had to spend time at the shop and Momma at her

job. Margaret was our constant companion, and we girls hated to leave her side. One week Daddy brought us a badminton set, and we all loved playing. Once again, we swam daily, took long hikes to the quarry, and explored the dirt roads for salamanders and other creatures. And at night the enchanting beacon. Summer visitors included Uncle George (Grandpa Joe's brother), Uncle Bill and Babe.

For two weeks that summer the photographer Connie Kanaga stayed with us.

Mary and Kitty
Delaware Water Gap
Summer, 1937

In lieu of room and board she took many portraits of Kitty and me, priceless images which we cherish to this day. In one snapshot from that summer, I see that Momma is checking my hair for lice.

Kitty and Mary, summer, 1937. Photo: Constance Kanaga

In the fall of 1937 our family moved to 20 Westminster Road, Brooklyn Heights, away from the Village for the first time. Although this apartment was cheap, airy, sunny, and large, it was an unhappy home. For one thing, the commute via bus and subway to Manhattan was long and arduous: Momma to midtown; Daddy, Kitty and I to the Village. Although I have many memories of this school, I have none of Brooklyn or of our long commutes.

One September day, after George walked out of the apartment saying he hated it there and would never return, Lucy wrote: "He is such a *taker*! If he never comes back I won't be surprised nor will I care very much once I get over it. He's weak and he's a parasite. Business is so terrible and George has no ambition to fix it." But after sleeping two nights in the book shop George returned to Brooklyn and—the usual pattern—they made up. Throughout the fall he frequently spent the night away from home. To this day, over seventy years later, I wonder where he was those nights. Would I have been as patient with him as Lucy was? Probably not.

Despite Lucy's constant concerns about money, they went out several evenings a week for drinks, meals, plays, movies, and art openings. That year they enjoyed Rogers and Hart's musical *Babes in Arms*, Steinbeck's drama *Of Mice and Men*, and the film *A Star is Born*. They took Kitty and me rowing in Central Park, to the Battery, to the zoo, to see *Snow White*, and bought us gypsy costumes, which we dearly loved.

92

Finally Lucy, realizing she could do little or nothing to change George, decided to change herself. She took a course in Public Speaking at Cooper Union, and got her hair cut and styled, "receiving many compliments." She thought of writing a weekly column for the Western Newspaper Union, and submitted this sample:

OUR NEW YORK by Lucile D. Kirk

We love it!

We've lived here for more than ten years. We've had lots of fun, and lots of headaches, but we still love it. Many of our friends have gone back home, to the small town, the middle-sized city, and to the suburbs. But we stay on.

We lived in a pretty big city until we came here, and we had also lived in the country and in small towns. (I'll never forget those small town experiences when I traveled with Chautauqua years ago! Nor the one year I spent away from home at a state university [Miami] in a small college town. Those *were* highly enjoyable.)

While George sells books I have one of the most fascinating jobs in the world on one of the national magazines. Every month I cover New York for events that will interest our readers.

One night it's a Broadway opening. I am not sophisticated, and when I feel it in my bones that the play hasn't a chance, I practically tremble with grief for the poor actors, for the trusting backer who has sunk a fortune (sometimes quite sizable) into a flop. *But* when the play sparkles, and the audience is held spellbound—that's a different story!

Comes an opening at an art gallery or one of the museums. I'm there. When the marvelous exhibit of the Italian masters opened at the Metropolitan Museum I practically risked life and limb in the swirling crowds to glimpse each of the twenty-eight old (and I mean old) masters. Titian's *Pope Paul*, the weary strong old man, with beautiful red robes; the matchless *Birth of Venus* by Botticelli. That lovely girl rises most gracefully from a clam shell!

I am no critic of either art or music, in the sense of having made a life-work of watching for flaws and imperfections. Quite the contrary. Is it pleasing? Do I enjoy it? That is my criterion for art, music, dance, theater, conversation, and food.

At least one evening a week I spend at a broadcast, another at a concert, a third and fourth at special events. Dining out is part of the job too, and right now this woman is paying. (When I went to buy a dress recently in my usual size sixteen [note: Lucy crossed out 'sixteen' and replaced it with 'fourteen'], I noticed a tendency to bulge where it was certainly not becoming. A cut in diet—just a wee one—and a trip to my favorite masseuse will do the trick in three or four weeks. I hope!)

I like to share. And I'd like to share my week's discoveries in New York with you. Won't you let me? And won't you write to me and tell me what you would like to hear about this big city's attractions?

Unfortunately, nothing came of this effort.

In November 1937 George and Lucy voted for Fiorello LaGuardia, who became one of the best, most liberal, mayors New York ever had, their first and last time of deviating from their socialist/democratic convictions. Later that month, when Bill and Myrtle O'Neil came to celebrate George's thirty-ninth birthday, Momma wrote: "Kids go nuts over O'Neil's." After a splendid Thanksgiving dinner at Mary Tobin's—accompanied by too much alcohol—Lucy and George fought hard, and Lucy ripped his pants. Once again, George left for the night.

Along with steady, reliable Harvey Brewer, they worked hard at the book shop during the holiday season, sometimes staying there all night and sleeping all morning. The card sales were good, and helped their finances considerably. Momma saw that Christmas was magical for us children. We were thrilled to see Santa at Wanamaker's, New York's elegant red-carpeted store; to see *Pinocchio*, and delighted with our holiday gifts. I turned four on Christmas Day.

Reading Lucy's diaries, I can't help wondering when that "happy-go-lucky lovely time" was and where that "charmed spot" was that they loved so much. It certainly was not Westminster Road, Brooklyn. And the time certainly was not 1938, a year that brought its own major problems and ushered in the beginning of the end of the Chelsea Book Shop.

In January 1938 Lucy wrote: "We've been careless about sex. I hope and pray for freedom from such an ordeal again. I will *not* have another baby by GK." And yet she would not have another abortion either. What to do? A visit to Dr. Shields proved that although her fears were unwarranted, she was once again suffering from nervous exhaustion. A sedative helped, and she wrote: "Life is mad, glorious, beautiful."

And then one February night, jumping up to close a window, Momma broke her right big toe. Although she was in much pain, no operation was called for. Instead she wore a splint with a loose, open shoe. She wrote: "Babes are so precious, dear. Little darling girls are so concerned." Later that month, on February 22, her beloved grandmother Kitty Ackley—who had been bedridden for years with a "bad hip"—died: "the sweetest, dearest, sanest person I ever knew," wrote Lucy. She was sad because her broken toe and financial constraints kept her from attending the funeral.

Further problems. After her toe healed, Lucy spent a week in Atlantic City covering a story for *School Management*. On her return George announced that he never came home during her absence, thus leaving Kitty and me alone with Margaret. Then, because book shop income was almost nil, he had to let stalwart Harvey go. Lucy wrote: "GK is so behind in his work and does so little about it….He's indolent, lazy, and shirks responsibility. This marriage will soon end." They decided to separate for a month, but they never did. Then Lucy decided to divorce him, but she never did this either. He promised to go "on the wagon," and she promised she'd pretend they were just married, but neither resolve lasted.

On March 25 Lucy wrote: "Life begins! I'm 40. Nice day at the office. Receive daffodils, violets, lilies. Thirteen take me out for cocktails. GK was to buy me a dictionary, I thought. Does not appear until 2:30. Brings me nothing."

At the end of March Margaret quit, giving no explanation. In desperate need, Lucy hired Alvira, the only person she interviewed. Alvira, the first black person Kitty and I had ever known, instilled fear in us: "If you don't behave the debil's gonna come and sit at the foot of your bed, and then if you're still bad he'll *eat you up*!" The latter said with great emphasis and force. She vividly described the debil's red body, pointed ears, and pitchfork. I was scared to death of him, never having heard of such evil before. Although I begged: "Momma, please don't have that Alvira for my maid. She scolds too much," Alvira stayed.

Lest you think otherwise, our lives were not totally bleak. Our parents took us to Coney Island, to Prospect Park, to Jacob Riis Park, the Brooklyn Botanical Gardens, and the Bronx Zoo. After seeing the baby animals there I wept, saying "I want to be born again." Best of all, Momma took us to the Barnum and Bailey Circus at Madison Square Garden. Oh how we loved the trapeze artists and the clowns. She wrote: "A superb time with the darling little girls." I'm ashamed to admit that Kitty and I brought home painted turtles destined to have short, miserable lives.

But trouble was ahead. Their dear friend Bob Mann, only 40, died suddenly of an aneurism. And Lucy, for the first time, was hospitalized with bursitis in her right shoulder. When she recovered, and when school was out for the summer, she packed Kitty and me up and we boarded the train to Cleveland. She remained there with us for two weeks, and although we pleaded to return with her, she left us there once again, in the care of our loving grandparents. The simple fact: our parents simply could not afford to keep us in New York. Grandma knew just what to do to make us happy: she took us to Higbee's and bought us each a pair of white Mary Jane's with cutouts.

Back in Brooklyn, although George and Lucy spent "a great July 4th, mostly in each other's arms," life was falling apart. Lucy discovered another suspicious note in his pocket. Mr. Hecht, upset by her two week absence, threatened to suspend *School Management*, and thus greatly reduce her job. Mr. St. John, said it was George's last month of renting 58 West 8th, as he owed more than $2,000 in rent. What to do? Leave the city altogether and buy a small house at the Delaware Water Gap? Move to Chicago, where Lucy was offered a job editing *Safety Education*? Close the book shop forever? This thought frightened Lucy more than it frightened George. Although he was ready to throw in the towel, she knew he'd be lost without the shop.

They decided to give the shop one more try. On August first, 1938, they rented a vacant store at 101 Greenwich Avenue (Greenwich and 12th Street), half the size of the old shop. With the help of many friends, they packed up and moved the stock. But the shop was robbed before it was officially re-opened, and many valuable books were stolen. Then the bank shut down the shop's account because of too many overdrafts. Things were going from bad to woise.

"I tremble at the prospect of no shop for him, but business is nil. Debts pile up. The CBS is a mess....I have great misgivings. GK is through!"

A Tiny Shop; a Big Disaster

In late August 1938 Lucy devised a budget, setting the total monthly expenses at $393. And setting the total monthly income in this way: her salary: $183; book shop: $210. The book shop income was totally unrealistic, as it actually brought in about $30 a month. As was so often the case, the gap between Lucy's expectations and reality was a certain recipe for disappointment and anger—usually directed towards George.

Grandma brought Kitty and me back to New York in early September: "They look wonderful and are so sweet. I bless their dear stalwart little hearts," wrote Momma. We came to a new apartment with a glassed-in porch at 13 Charles Street, back in our beloved Village. Momma placed an ad for childcare in *The New York Times*, and selected Jesse Newell, a woman Kitty and I came to love. Daddy surprised us with Aphra Behn, an adorable gray and white kitten. Since the name of the first professional woman writer in English meant nothing to us, we girls called her "Aferbane."

At first I was happy to return to the Little Red Schoolhouse, but soon started a strike, and refused to attend. I kicked, cried, and threw tantrums so my parents would keep me at home. Here's why. When the teacher (I cannot remember her name) gave us a 1/2 pint carton of milk each morning she provided no

Mary, October, 1938
Photo: Consuela Kanaga

99

straw; I invariably spilled mine and was ashamed and embarrassed. Only after Momma convinced her to let me use a straw was I willing to return.

The same teacher was concerned about my speech, which was still difficult to understand, although I was oblivious to the problem. I started telling people they were just one great big handkerchief, and my parents thought this was cute and funny. At a conference my teacher set them straight; "Oh, I'm so very sorry. She picked that up from the other children. Don't you know what Mary's saying? She's saying: 'You're just one great big hunk of shit.'"

Our parents did their very best for us. They took us on the Staten Island ferry and to Central Park Zoo, where we had our first pony rides. They gave us dancing lessons at Bea White's. I remember well the thrill of buying ballet slippers at the Capezio store. Kitty was graceful and modest, while I was clumsy and proud. In November Momma took us to Wanamaker's again, where we walked up the magnificent red-carpeted staircase to find Santa on the mezzanine, alongside a pianist playing Christmas carols. O how thrilling that was! Then we rode the elevator to the top floor for a fancy lunch at the store's elegant restaurant.

In late November, when Daddy turned forty, I cried because there was no cake for him. Dear Jessie baked him one, and Momma borrowed $100 to help with book shop expenses. His Cleveland friend Howard Wolf visited, and Momma generously told them to "go out and make a night of it," which they did. After that Daddy went on the wagon again, and Momma wrote: "I'm so proud of GK....He's so much nicer this way. He's not drinking and he admits to feeling better."

But even with Daddy working hard and Momma helping when she could, Christmas season at the new location was a disaster. There were almost no sales, even of holiday cards.

Although the new location was only a few blocks from West 8th, customers were reluctant to cross 7th Avenue to get there. The shop had no charm and Daddy had neither the money nor the ambition to fix it up.

To make matters worse, a U.S. Marshall posted a notice on the door. Daddy had a judgment of over $500 past due, and only a week to pay the hundreds owed at 58 West 8th. The phone company disconnected the shop's service. Try as they might, they could not make the back payments. Momma was furious with him for making so little effort: "I've got to talk separation, as life with him is no joy. I descry his vile secretive mood....I'm really getting to hate and despise him." She told him to stay away for a week, and wanted to either separate or start anew. But once again, he vowed to change, and for a while came home promptly for meals and for the night. Walter Goldwater, a kind bookseller and friend, realizing our family's plight, offered Daddy part-time work.

Despite their dire financial straits, I am amazed by the extent to which they continued their social life: cocktails, dinners out, and the theatre. Lucy continued with weekly massages, hair styling, and restaurant lunches. Obviously, and perhaps importantly so, entertainment and personal care remained high priorities.

Kitty and I, oblivious to our family's problems, were happy with school, with dancing, and with Jessie. At Christmastime our parents took us in a taxi to see the spectacular lights up Fifth Avenue, the tree at Rockefeller Center, and to *Hansel and Gretel*. When a friend of theirs gave us peasant costumes Momma said we were "delirious with joy."

Kitty and Mary, for 1938 Christmas card
Photo: Consuela Kanaga

All seemed well. But then Jessie "had an incident" and had to be rushed to Bellevue. Later we learned that she was paranoid/schizophrenic, and could have murdered us all. I turned five on Christmas Day.

Momma hired Joe, a kind gay man, to care for Kitty and me during the day, and Anna Higgins, "a true treasure," to help at night. But our parents really couldn't afford to keep us, and so in mid-February, after Daddy bought us all chocolate hearts, Momma once again took us to our Cleveland grandparents.

Things got worse in New York. Some days George, demoralized and floundering, didn't even go near the book shop. He didn't love it as he had loved the shop on West 8th, in fact he didn't even like it, and he saw no way out. The electricity in their apartment was cut off because of unpaid bills. They tried to sub-let two rooms, but found no tenants. Lucy wrote: "He has given me no money since Christmas. He won't let me manage the money. It just slips through his fingers. So cross! He hasn't a nickel to his name: can't even get his shirts from the chinks." Their friend Judge Bertha Schwartz suggested he file for bankruptcy. Instead he took a part-time temporary job helping sort books for a dealer in Long Island City. Lucy wrote him a note:

> May 10, 1939. 13 Charles Street
>
> Too bad.
>
> It's probably because we just don't love each other *enough*. My fault for not being able to accept you as you are... careless about your person, so much of the time unshaven; careless about keeping appointments with others as well as with me; careless about phoning when late; careless about coming to meals on time. And practically reprehensible about getting up and getting to bed.
>
> Through all these years together I am conscious of a deepening disappointment in you as I, against what I want to believe, find you lacking in personal integrity and in moral

stamina. Find you almost reprehensible where money and debt are concerned. Maybe a little worry and regret, but a shrug of the shoulders, a lift of the eyebrow, and it is so easily dismissed by you.

Deeper and deeper do I feel your lack of interest in and affection for your children. Your complete indifference to their health, welfare, schooling. Your unwillingness to sacrifice personal small pleasures of smoking and drinking (you are so much better on this score that I am indiscreet in mentioning it here) to buy them a toy, me a flower.

I can't accept you as you are. *You* must make the effort at change if we are to be together next fall. You must put forth the effort for a united family, for pleasant home relationships.

After that George tried, at least for a while. Soon Grandma brought us back to New York, and Momma wrote: "They are the *darlingist* children." Kitty, now seven, went to the Little Red Schoolhouse Camp for two weeks, while Grandma and I stayed with the Al Fishers' at their country home. After that we had a magical day at the New York World's Fair, where we marveled at the Trilon and Hemisphere, the multi-colored strobe lights and the breathtaking pavilions. Then we spent weeks at the Delaware Water Gap, and once again were happy there.

But what to do with us girls in the fall? Lucy wrote: "Now to plan for the hard, lean year ahead. Shall we send the babes back to Ohio? I want to do best by the children. Though it breaks my heart, I believe that's the most sensible plan." Our parents took us rowing in Prospect Park, down to Battery Park, and to the Aquarium. But early one morning in mid-September we once again boarded the train for Cleveland. There, after I cried and cried for our beloved cat Aphra Behn, our parents shipped her to us; I imagine at great expense.

George wasn't ready to just give up on the shop. "He's crazy about the book business, if only it would make some money," wrote Lucy. All our relatives knew our family was in crisis, and several sent money. When the apartment's electricity was cut off once again, Lucy slept at the Waldorf, while George slept at the shop. In late September they moved to a single room at 51 West 10th Street, which had no shelves for dishes or books.

And then the dream of owning a book shop in Greenwich Village and of leading a bohemian, carefree life came to an abrupt and harsh end. The economic times, George's carelessness with money, the unexpected children, the expenses of our illnesses, and the forced move to Greenwich Avenue were insurmountable factors. Lucy wrote: "I tremble at the prospect of no shop for him, but business is nil. Debts pile up. The CBS is a mess."

In the fall of 1939, World War II began full force: Germany invaded Poland; Franco took Madrid; Italy invaded Albania; Russia invaded Finland. In September England and France declared war on Germany. Roosevelt pledged neutrality.

And back at home, on September 27th, almost the entire stock of the Chelsea Book Shop went up for sale at the National Book Auction. Much to George's dismay, the sale brought in almost nothing. Lucy wrote: "I have great misgivings. *GK is through!*" Although he half-heartedly tried selling last year's Christmas cards, a few weeks later Lucy wrote: "I'm so tired of GK not doing *anything*. Unless I put my foot right down he'll drift forever. I won't have it. Will speak tonight and get him out job-hunting Monday."

At ninety, Mother wrote down her feelings about the closing of the book shop:

"Very sad. We loved that little shop. In 1938 we did not want to sign a lease, as business was poor. So we were there on a month to month basis. Along came Marlboro, a successful remainder outlet, who offered

1939

BOOK SALE

Our whole stock of books at absurdly low prices.

Thousands formerly 50c to $1.50
now at 39c

Chelsea Book Shop

101 Greenwich Ave.   (Next door to Greenwich Theatre)
CHelsea 3-2731   Hours 10 to 10

RENTAL LIBRARY   BOOKS BOUGHT AND SOLD
DISTINCTIVE GREETING CARDS

CHELSEA BOOK SHOP
58 WEST 8th STREET
NEW YORK CITY
Tel. SPring 7-1382

Mr. St. John "double what Kirk is paying," and we were out. Because Christmas season—November and December—were out best time of year, we moved to the only vacant store available, 101 Greenwich Avenue. But even moving four or five blocks away lost us many, many customers. It was a tiny shop and a big disaster. Not half or a fourth of the customer traffic of our beloved 8th Street. It was no real surprise that GK gave up the store. We were completely out in the fall of 1939. And that began a bad period for George. We kept the CBS through the Depression. How? I'll never know. Good library business, but used books were not in demand. Lower 4th Avenue had scores of book shops, including Walter Goldwater's."

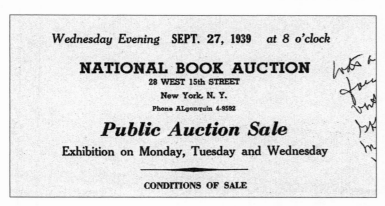

The truth is, the Chelsea Book Shop would not have lasted a year without Lucy. She was pretty, gay, and out-going; some customers came in just to be around her. Against her will and her natural inclinations, but because of necessity, she became the practical, responsible business person, insisting on handling the money. She established the popular lending library and insisted on selling seasonal greeting cards. Although George balked at both, considering them "Babbittry," he had to admit they brought in much-needed income. "He was," wrote Lucy, "first and foremost a bookman, and he should have married a wealthy woman, which I was not."

At Christmastime 1939 our parents came to Cleveland for a week. Kitty and I had no idea of the troubles they'd been through and, as always, were delighted to see them. On Christmas Day Momma wrote: "Our sweetie pie Mary is six and she is working hard at it—eating and drinking and dressing quicker." Grandpa Joe, who had been in the hospital and was scheduled for surgery, came home for a few days.

It was a happy, celebratory time, which did not last. Three weeks later, on January 14, Grandpa Joe, at 70, died of uremic poisoning after his non-cancerous prostate operation. Kitty and I missed him terribly. Every morning he used to walk to the Czech bakery for fresh poppy-seed rolls which he served us for breakfast, along with hot coffee in our milk to warm us up.

Mr. Hecht, the publisher of *Parents'*, gave Momma $150 and a week's vacation to return to Cleveland for her father's funeral. When she visited Grandpa's drugstore at Broadway and 49th she wrote: "Feels so natural and sweet at the old store. We feel our dad so much!" She also met with our teachers and said they were "lavish in their praise." When she returned to New York she left us with her despondent, exhausted mother.

Back in New York she was able to put much of her sorrow aside: "GK is a perfect darling. Offered to keep Dad's store going. Gosh, do I love him!" They continued their active social life and made several more trips to the World's Fair. When guests arrived from Cleveland Lucy wrote: "The darlingest GK bakes us a handsome custard pie, though he rolled out the crust on a cookie tin with a can of beans."

In March the tide turned. "Found a lovely new vanity in GK's overcoat pocket and thought it was for me, but he hasn't given it to me yet." And, alas, he never did. Lucy had a tooth pulled, which not only formed a dry socket, but also left an open hole into her sinus cavity, a problem which plagued her for the rest of her life. She felt "punk" with an undiagnosed rash and a fever of 102. She worried because her periods were irregular. She felt she was getting fat and vowed to walk to work, to have no more cocktails and no more second helpings. She wrote: "I want my children; I want George to support himself and them. If he can't, I'm probably out…not because he has no job, but because he doesn't work day and night toward getting one. I'm probably the world's most discouraged woman right now." Con Edison cut off their electricity. George was reading through Shakespeare's plays.

But then Lucy, being Lucy, bounced back. She took a course at New York University on magazine writing. She joined Theta Sig, the Women's Journalism

Sorority. She sent out two query letters daily, hoping for additional work. And then George was offered part-time work helping another bookseller.

In June, much to our delight, Momma came to Cleveland for a month. She took us to see Bob Hope at the Palace. She wrote: "Sweet sleeping babes so lovely. They awaken me with 'Momma Derioca.' We play all day." Momma had an important mission on that trip: she asked Grandma Ada to live with us in New York. Grandma said yes, but only on one condition; that she could help raise Kitty and me. How wonderful that was for all of us. Years later Mother wrote: "We all loved having her. We paid her the modest sum we could scarcely afford, but I owe her a million."

Grandma Ada with Mary and Kitty Lakewood Ohio, June 1940

On Lucy's return to New York, miracle of miracles, George was offered the perfect job: managing Barnes & Noble's used book shop. In August they moved to a fifth floor apartment at 457 West 123rd Street, six light-filled rooms, at $60 a month. George received a raise from Mr. Barnes.

When Grandma, Kitty and I arrived in New York in early September, only Daddy met us at Grand Central. Once again, Momma was hospitalized with an attack of bursitis. We came to the new apartment in an unfamiliar part of Manhattan, and Grandma, at 64, began a completely new life. On her return from the hospital, Momma wrote; "Babes are such darlings!" After spending another lovely day at the World's Fair, we enrolled as "scholarship children" at Horace Mann—the lab school for Columbia's Teachers' College—Kitty in the third grade, and I in the second. Momma registered for graduate courses at Teachers' College. She wrote: "Life looks rosy. I love this fall."

Lucy and George, Christmas, 1959. Photo: Axel Blomberg

Part Three

LAST TIMES

*"Carpe Diem, kid! That's all there is;
there ain't no more."*

Not for Me, the Spring

New Year's Eve, 1961. Only my father and I stay up to see the New Year in. My baby Stephen, Mother and Grandma have been long asleep. Kitty, now a mother too, is with her new family in Cleveland. We sit in green wing-back chairs on either side of the fireplace. Only the fire, the blinking bulbs on the tree, and the candles on the table between us light the room. In an uncertain world, with Russian missiles on Cuba, with Americans building bomb shelters and hoarding food, this house in Pelham, New York—which our family bought in 1945—is a place of safety and peace.

The fire highlights Daddy's white hair and his handsome, kindly face. He wears a plaid flannel shirt and tan corduroys which, because of his recent operation, now hang loose and require suspenders. His are red.

On the table between us lies our midnight feast: lobster tails with melted butter, toast squares, oranges, a bowl of unshelled nuts, and a bottle of André champagne.

The flames light the bookshelves flanking the fireplace, and the Homer and Breughel prints, the map of Prague, and the Bellows watercolor of children playing in Central Park, which hang on the turquoise walls.

I have come to New York with my infant son to see how Daddy is doing, and more specifically, to fix up his room for his period of convalescence. I placed his favorite books in the wall to wall bookcases, some unlikely bedfellows: Dostoyevsky between Dickens and Euripides; Sophocles between Shakespeare and Swinburne; Wilde between Whitman and Zola—well, maybe that combination wasn't so unlikely—hauled in a large desk, bought a used typewriter, an Indian spread for his single bed, and hung bright curtains. I don't remember when he moved from the master bedroom to this small back room. Probably the last time Mother threatened divorce.

While he's recovering, I'm hoping he'll write about the years in New York before marriage when, as a member of the Kalem Club, he was friends with many writers, and about the years he owned the Chelsea Book Shop in Greenwich Village.

When he saw how I had changed his room Daddy seemed pleased with everything but my arrangement of the books: "Never push them back like that, kiddo. Books stay out level with the shelves, so we can read their spines easily. But I appreciate the thought anyway, sweetheart," he said.

I am relieved to see how well he looks, and to hear, directly from Dr. Birnkrant, that they "got everything." Now only a few weeks' recuperation, and then he'll be back to work as a lathe operator at Precision Tool Company. It's a good job. For years, Mother, as an editor of *Parents' Magazine*, was the main support of our family. Although it pains me that Daddy's now a factory worker; after many years of unemployment, or part-time menial jobs, he's happy with this work. I am amazed that he could learn this trade so well, but often forget he spent his junior year at Mechanic's High. And then he quit school. If he's happy, why shouldn't I be?

I live in Minneapolis because my husband, Eric, is a PhD candidate at the University of Minnesota. I teach 12th grade English at Central High, where we have just finished a poetry unit. We ended with the Pound Canto: "What thou lovest well remains, the rest is dross./ What thou lovest well shall not be reft from thee." I quote these lines to Daddy, and, although unable to identify them, he repeats them verbatim.

His brush with death made teaching this unit more poignant. The Tennyson and Stevenson poems about death, Dickinson, and Pound, all reminded me of the mortality of someone I love so deeply. I love literature, I love teaching, I love Stephen, Eric, Kitty, Grandma, and Mother very deeply also, but I have a special bond with Daddy. Why is that? Probably because I've always taken his side against Mother. Whenever she filed for divorce, he refused to sign the papers, saying he felt it would be unhealthy for the family. Mother doesn't understand that if only she were nicer to him, Daddy wouldn't drink so much. She even makes him wash out his own socks and underwear. How humiliating! I feel protective of him, even sorry for him, as for one who cannot defend himself. I'm the only one who really understands him.

I don't know how to broach the question that sizzles on my tongue, but I am determined to ask it tonight. After our champagne toast at midnight, "To life, and to each other," I get up my nerve. "Daddy, what do you believe happens after death?" I lean forward in anticipation of his answer.

He sings: "The bells in hell go ting-a-ling-a-ling/ for you but not for me.../ O Death where is thy sting-a-ling-a-ling?/ O Grave thy mystery?"

"Come on, Daddy, be serious for once!"

He reaches across the table and takes my hands in his: "Carpe Diem, kid. That's all there is: there ain't no more."

I, still young and in my hopeful stage, am disappointed and saddened, but try not to show it. I *want* there to be more, but growing up in this non-religious household, I have trouble believing there is. I remind him of Grandma's certainty that she and Grandpa Joe will be re-united in death. For her sake, I hope it's so.

But he just shakes his head: "Nix. She might think she'll see him again, but it ain't necessarily so. In fact, it ain't so."

I have to let it go. We revert to our favorite subject: literature. He loves Whitman, and quotes "Song of Myself"—"I celebrate myself and sing myself/ and what I assume you shall assume/ for every atom belonging to me/ as good belongs to you."

"Oh, Whitman's so me, me, me!" I say, not yet appreciating the wonder of his poetry. "But Dickinson, she didn't even want to be noticed. And she was every bit as good. Maybe better."

"Dickinson?" Daddy says. "She had skim milk in her veins, and who can celebrate skim milk? Nothing to notice, nothing to celebrate. Give old Walt another chance." And I will, because he suggests it. He knows more about literature than anyone I've ever met.

"When school resumes," I say, "we'll start a unit in drama: *Lear*, *Death of a Salesman*, and *The Glass Menagerie*. I'm excited about teaching these plays. What do you think?"

"What do I think, kiddo? You know what I think. Stick to the Elizabethans: Shakespeare and Marlowe. I'll bet you've never even read *The Jew of Malta*! It's time, kid, it's time. But *Lear* now. That play is first rate. Nothing touches it."

And so the conversation goes, easy back and forth.

Soon the champagne's gone, the food consumed, the fire flickering, and it's well after 1:00. I start to gather the dishes. We're leaving early in the morning. It's time to say good-night, and maybe good-bye until the spring. "Daddy, I'll be back during Easter break. Let's plan a day of fishing then, just like old times."

"Seems Like Old Times," Daddy whistles, and I happily join in: "Old times/ having you to walk with/ Old times/ having you to talk with."

"When are you coming back home, I mean for good?" he asks.

"When Eric finishes his PhD we'll come back, so I can be near you," I smile at him. We've been away for a long time: first two years in Cleveland, where Eric began graduate school, and now almost three in Minneapolis. We have every intention of returning to New York, our home.

"How can you stand that god-forsaken place?" Daddy asks, for the hundredth time. He has never been to Minnesota.

We embrace, ready to part. "At any rate, I'll see you soon," I say.

Daddy shakes his head slowly: "Sweetheart, I'll quote Pushkin: 'Not for me, the spring.'"

Oh, I wish he weren't such a tease. "Quit kidding!" I say, as I pull away to look at him, knowing he's being his humorous self. But his face is serious and sad. I can't hold back my tears.

Daddy takes me in his arms: "Whatever happens to me, sweetheart, promise me you'll take good care of your Mother." I nod. He tightens his embrace: "It's okay, kiddo, really, it's okay. You'll be fine, just fine."

Back in Minneapolis, I think about Daddy's years since losing the book shop. The Barnes & Noble job lasted less than a year. Mr. Barnes let him go, saying he'd never hire him again, but I don't know why. Then Daddy attended Mechanics' Institute and the School of Metal Trades, where he learned to be a lathe operator, a very marketable skill. First he worked nights at Sperry Gyroscope on Long Island and then days at Reed Instrument in Manhattan, but these wartime jobs ended in 1945. After that sometimes he sold books from home, sometimes he worked as a florist's helper, but usually was unemployed.

Although he continued to be a gracious and charming host, continued his love of books, of cats, and of all of us, family life was colored by his alcoholism, his inability to hold down a good job, and his nonchalant attitude towards being a responsible, reliable adult.

After Kitty and I married and left home (1955 and 1957 respectively,) financial pressures eased, and he and Mother grew closer again. They had memorable trips to Great Britain, Ireland, and Italy. He took up fishing, tied his own flies, and loved being outside alone all day. Finally Daddy found work he loved, as a lathe operator at Precision Instrument Company in Mount Vernon, where he was highly respected for his skills. When he was diagnosed with colon cancer, the company kept him on the payroll and gave him an extended leave of absence. He planned to return to work in January.

George at Harlech Castle in North Wales, 1961.

On March 21st, 1962, I am back in New York. Room 503 in the vast Manhattan General Hospital has three beds, each with a plastic chair and a bed stand beside it. Its walls are an ugly, institutional green. In the farthest bed, my father lies sleeping in a fetal position, facing the window. His hospital gown, open at the back, reveals a diaper. Mother sits in the chair beside him, holding his hand.

Only yesterday Mother phoned our apartment: "Your father has taken a sudden turn for the worse. I took him to the hospital and they kept him for observation. He's very weak. Dr. Birnkrant thinks his cancer may have returned. Could you possibly come?"

Could I possibly come? Of course I could. After my return to Minneapolis in January, just in case, I set up photos of Daddy: the pampered baby in a white dress, the frightened bridegroom, the confident bookseller, the father holding a child's hand as they cross the George Washington Bridge, the charming host carving a turkey, the proud father walking his daughter to her wedding.

After arranging care for Stephen, I flew to LaGuardia about noon today, took a taxi to Manhattan General, and went directly to room 503. I hold Mother to me. "Oh honey," she says, "how wonderful to see you. I'm so glad you're here. Thank you."

"It's the only place in the world I want to be," I assure her. I turn to Daddy.

"Hello, Daddy, it's me, your favorite daughter," I whisper in his ear, as I kiss his flushed cheek. It's very hot. I take his hand. It's very cold. His breathing is labored. He opens his eyes briefly. Does he smile ever so slightly? Does he know me? I'm not sure. The odor of urine is overpowering.

Soon a nurse who introduces herself as "Margie" bustles in with two aides: "Hello, dearie," she says to Daddy. "I see you've got your family here. How nice. It's a good thing we shaved you this morning." She turns to us: "Please leave the room while we clean up Mr. Kirk and give him his shot. I'll open the door when we're finished."

In the hallway, Mother says: "Oh, he looks so much better! We were worried about pneumonia, but George doesn't even need oxygen. He just has a cold."

When we re-enter, Daddy is sitting up, with the bed raised. They are adjusting his pillows. "We won't bother with the teeth tonight," the kind nurse says. "I know they're a nuisance for you."

"What was that shot for?" Mother asks Margie.

"To make things easier for him," she replies.

Now that Daddy is awake, Mother hugs him: "Geordie, how are you, sweetheart? Your color's back. You look wonderful. Look, I've brought you a surprise!" She turns to me.

"Is that you, kiddo?" He smiles weakly. "What brings you here?"

Mother touches my hand, meaning "Don't tell." I try to smile, but my face belies my words. I can't hide anything. I kiss his cheek and take his hand. "Oh, I had a few days off, so I thought I'd come see if you were behaving yourself."

"Got no choice," he tries to smile.

An orderly plops a dinner tray on the bed table and removes its brown plastic cover: "Enjoy, Mr. Kirk," he says. Dinner tonight consists of chicken broth, saltines, coffee, and lemon Jell-o with a dab of white stuff on top. Daddy dips a spoon into the broth but, too weak to hold it steady, spills it on his gown. After his second try, I sit on the bed and spoon some into his mouth. After a few sips, he shakes his head, and pushes back the tray. Coffee? Nix. Jell-O? "Nix. I never could stomach the stuff."

"Remember the meal we shared on New Year's Eve: lobster tails and champagne? I'll bet you would eat that," I say.

"Or maybe a cold beer and a hot pastrami," Daddy whispers, "but not this crap."

Mother takes his hand: "Geordie, please eat something. You have to get strong so I can bring you home."

Will she ever bring him home? Daddy had a couple of good months. In January he began work again, but soon was unable to keep going. In February Mother took him to Sanibel Island, where he could loaf. Photos from that trip show him thin, tan, and smiling as he proudly displays a string of fish. But when they returned home he continued downhill until now, when he's landed in the hospital.

George on Sanibel Island,
February 1962

Soon his head droops and his eyes won't stay open, so we prepare to leave.

Mother and I have an appointment the next morning with his doctor and old friend, Bill Birnkrant, and then we'll spend the day with Daddy. As Mother kisses him goodnight, he seems to rouse himself: "Lucy," he whispers hoarsely to Mother, "they want to stick a god-damned catheter up me and make me use a bed-pan. I can't. Jesus, you'd think I was on my death-bed! Tell Bill if I'm going to shit it's going to be in a toilet." Mother promises, cradles his head while she kisses him, and I cannot hear what they whisper to each other. She caresses his face with the back of her hand.

I'm so delighted by their tenderness toward each other, so glad Mother loves him again, so glad they had those European trips. I crank the bed back down and re-adjust his pillows. My summers long ago as a nurses' aide come in handy, and I know just what to do. I kiss him goodnight: "See you in the morning, Daddy. Sleep well."

"Arrivederci, kiddo," he says, "Take good care of your mother."

"Thank god he's getting better," says Mother, as we walk to the elevator. "How does he seem to you, sweetheart?"

"Pretty good, considering," I say, heartened by her words. Tomorrow I'll read to him and wheel him into the atrium. Maybe even outside if it's warm and sunny, as today. "Arrivederci," he said. Good-bye for now.

We go home to a late supper and a restful sleep.

The next morning, as we arrive at Bill Birnkrant's, he puts an arm around each of us and leads us into his office. "Lucy, Mary, I have terrible news for you. I am so sorry. The hospital just phoned; George never woke up this morning. He died peacefully in his sleep."

George in his mid-fifties
Photographer unknown

"George was a lovely lover, just lovely."

In a Better Place

"Let's have lunch at the best restaurant in New York and let's order martinis in George's honor," says Mother. She and I are in a taxi heading towards midtown from Campbell's Mortuary, where we have just delivered Daddy's clothing in a cardboard box. Campbell's required the clothes, because in Manhattan it is illegal to transport a naked body. I look at her in amazement. Just hours ago my father died in Manhattan General Hospital.

After sobbing and holding each other in Bill Birnkrant's office for heaven knows how long, we walked to the hospital where I gathered Daddy's clothing into a box provided for such purposes. Then, while Mother sat in the lobby, I phoned several funeral homes: "Just a plain wooden coffin. He'll be cremated," and decided on Campbell's. In the taxi up to the mortuary on East 81st Street I held the sad carton on my lap.

Mother lays her hand on mine: "Last night when I kissed George goodnight he told me to take care of you. But now you're taking care of me."

"We're taking care of each other," I say, squeezing her hand. Last night when I kissed Daddy goodnight he had whispered to me: "Arriverderci, kiddo. Take good care of your mother."

March 22, 1962, the first day of spring, and once again it is a yellow world. The trees are full of their green-gold leaf buds. Forsythia are in bloom. In another month it will be Easter. Mother holds the daffodils she bought for Daddy and the card she signed "To my Geordie from Lovin' Lu," pet names from their courtship.

It's after 2:00 when we arrive at The Cattleman on West 45th, and although only a few diners remain, we ask for a corner table. I sit on Mother's left and put my arm around her. Our waiter, who introduces himself as "Pierre", smiles as he lights the candle on our table: "And how are you lovely ladies today?"

Remembering Daddy's favorite gin, I order Smirnoff martinis and a basket of bread. The thought of alcohol on an empty stomach nauseates me. "What a day!" says Mother. "Well, George would want us to make the best of it." She fumbles with her glasses. "Bill says your father's in a better place now." I study the menu. "Do *you* think he's in a better place?" she asks me directly.

"Sure," I say, even though not a cell in my body believes this. "Yes, I'm sure he is." Pierre returns and I order lobster salads for us, remembering the many times Daddy and I shared lobster tails with melted butter. Mother orders a second martini. Although she will soon be sixty-four, Mother is still beautiful and vibrant. She wears a houndstooth suit, silver pin and earrings, and a wide-brimmed hat; just as if it were a regular day and she were on her way to work at *Parents'*. Strands of her carefully upswept hair hang lank around her face.

She lays her hand on mine, and the topaz ring made of Daddy's birthstones sparkles: "You know, dear, if I had it all to do over again, I'd still marry him." She sips her martini. "And then I'd divorce him." She takes a bite of salad. "But then I'd marry him again.

Lucy, 1965.

I wouldn't trade my life with him for anything. Those early years in the book shop were our happiest." I squeeze her hand, knowing she means the years before Kitty and I were born. After a minute or so she muses: "I wonder if I'll ever see him again." I can't answer this one.

We play with our food in silence, and when Mother drops her fork she almost falls off her chair trying to retrieve it. Pierre rushes over to help and I ask for the check. I need to get her home. "I've lost my appetite, sweetheart," Mother says. "I'm tired, so very tired, dear. Can we go home now?" Out of habit, she takes out a mirror, powders her face, and applies fresh lipstick. "George was a lovely lover, just lovely," she says, her face distorted now, and tears rolling down her cheeks.

I turn and take her in my arms: "It's okay, Momma, really it's okay. You'll be fine, just fine." As I hold her I'm astonished by my words. It's been many, many years since I've called my mother "Momma." She leaves the daffodils on the table, and I guide her across Fifth Avenue towards Grand Central.

And that day, fifty years ago, seems like yesterday. And Mother's death, eighteen years ago, seems like this morning. And here I am at seventy-eight reliving these moments etched indelibly in my memory.

Postscript: The reader may wonder where my sister Kitty was during these days. She had arrived in New York (from Chicago) before I did, saw Daddy, and was almost immediately hospitalized with a serious ear infection which required delicate surgery. That evening Mother and I visited her, recuperating in New Rochelle Hospital, to convey our sad news.

"Your mother was a beautiful woman with much savvy. She always wore high heels and, with those long slim legs, was lovely to look at. Thank God women didn't wear slacks back then."

Old Times

"Oh, Lucy, those were the best days, weren't they?" Harvey Brewer asks Mother.

"The best days of my life; just swell," says Mother, and Harvey puts his arm around her and draws her to him. They are old, old friends, the oldest of friends, who love each other dearly. My sister Kitty and I, sitting across the table, look at each other and smile. We have become excess baggage. I love seeing these two beloved people so happy to be together again.

It is June 1988, and Kitty and I have brought Mother to New York for her 90th birthday celebration. We are staying at the Hotel Wyndham on West 57th Street, across from Central Park. Harvey came by for us this morning bringing violet corsages. Now he is treating us to an elegant brunch at the Plaza Hotel. Mother has groomed herself carefully for this reunion, penciling in her thin eyebrows, applying lipstick and rouge, piling up her brown hair with combs and bobby pins. She wears a lavender knit top, navy slacks, black lace-up shoes, and purple pin and earrings.

Lucy with her friend Harvey Brewer at the Hotel Wyndham, New York City, 1988.

The spacious dining room has a black and white checkerboard floor and gilt mirrors. There are gleaming white tablecloths and fresh bouquets on each table. In the northwest corner a man plays Cole Porter and Gershwin on a grand piano. Catching my reflection, I realize I should have dressed more mindfully: worn the sleeveless black dress instead of the Global Village lavender skirt and blue cotton top. We had hoped to see Alice, Harvey's wife, but know she's been ill for several months. Mother asks tentatively: "Tell me, *how* is Alice?"

Harvey withdraws his arm from Mother's shoulders. Before replying, he fumbles in his pocket for a handkerchief and wipes his eyes: "Lucy, I buried her two days ago."

"Oh, no!" exclaims Mother. We are all shocked, and express our sorrow with various exclamations. Alice was a quiet, gentle and kind woman, a fine pianist and an avid birder. I thought she was elegant. She and Harvey, with no children of their own, doted on Kitty and me. Of course we loved her. "How could you possibly meet with us today? You should have called and postponed it," says Mother. She has forgotten that the day of Daddy's death we had lunch at The Cattleman.

"I needed to see you, Lucy," Harvey said. "I knew it would do me a world of good to be with you and the girls. And it already has."

And it does Mother a world of good to see Harvey also. Her face, which lit up with sheer pleasure when they greeted each other, is still glowing. She has been widowed for over twenty-five years, and Harvey for only a week. "Seems like old times," she says, patting his knee. And the time they're remembering is indeed old; over fifty years ago.

"You were just a boy in knee pants when you started to work for us. Do you remember?" asks Mother. "You were so inquisitive, and had a fine instinct for old books. And your father drew that wonderful map for us."

"Of course I remember, Lucy. And now I'm an old, old man. And everything I know about the book business I learned from you and George." Once again he puts his arm around Mother. "Just think, Lucy, I worked there for eleven years. You two were like my surrogate parents." Mother looks at him quizzically. "Or more like my big brother and sister." Mother smiles. "Anyway, my mentors. George taught me about books. You taught me about people. Those old times were the best times, weren't they?" He and Mother smile at each other. "More champagne?" He refills our glasses and orders another bottle.

When the Chelsea Book Shop closed in 1939, Harvey was twenty-six and newly married. He and Alice moved to Closter, New Jersey, where he made a living the rest of his life selling art books, fine prints, and old maps.

"And dear, dear Alice," says Mother. "You met her at our book shop too, didn't you? She walked in wearing that chipmunk coat, and George called her 'Chippie' right from the first. Do you remember?"

"Of course I remember." Harvey turns to Kitty and me, and once again relates the story of their courtship: "Her mother asked her why she made such frequent visits to the book shop. Was it that tall, dark, very handsome man? Nope, it was me." We laugh, once again loving this familiar story and this charming man. "We were married over fifty years," Harvey adds. "She was my best friend."

There are two kinds of New Yorkers: the showy, self-conscious ones and the slouchy, comfortable ones. I suspect the former kind and love the latter. Harvey is slouchy and relaxed, with long arms and legs, a little disheveled, smiling, easygoing, sophisticated, and has that endearing accent. Although only in his seventies, he looks nearly as old as Mother, perhaps from years of smoking. His white hair is parted on the side. He has a large nose, kind blue eyes, and a skeptical, knowing expression. Oblivious to his elegant surroundings, he wears a shiny blue-gray suit, white socks, and a plaid, open-necked sports shirt.

"Your mother was a beautiful woman with much savvy," Harvey says to Kitty and me. "She always wore high heels and, with those long slim legs, was lovely to look at. Thank God women didn't wear slacks then." He touches Mother's arm affectionately, and they both smile as they look down at her roomy slacks and her lace-up flats. "It wasn't so much fun after you left to work at *Parents'*, but then of course I had Alice's legs to admire."

Mother becomes young again as she and Harvey reminisce about the book shop customers: enormous Mr. French, the Valentine man, Dr. Fralick the cadger. They have lots to talk about: bathtub gin, Daddy's arrest for speeding, the robbery, the greeting cards, the lending library, the old neighborhood.

"And then the children came," says Harvey. "How you and George adored them!" He turns to Kitty: "You were such a serious child with big eyes and dark hair." He turns to me: "And you were a tousle-headed blonde whose face would light up on seeing your Daddy." Then back to Mother: "Alice and I hoped for children just like yours, but as they say, I shot only empty bullets."

Mother changes the subject: "Yesterday I had lunch with Ramona Lazare." Harvey inquires about her, and they reminisce about her husband Eddie, who worked at the book shop for many years and then went on to edit *The American Bookman* and *American Book Prices Current*. He too has been dead many years.

"And Monday the girls took me down to the old shop on West 8th," Mother tells Harvey. "Now it's an herbal supplement store run by two nice young men. I told them we used to own a book shop there and that as a bride I lived on the fourth floor front. They let us into the courtyard, which hasn't changed. That old stone bench is still there. Oh, those lovely times!"

We photographed Mother sitting on that bench, smiling as if she remembered all the charm and happiness of her young self, and of her newly-married life. I could almost see Daddy sitting there beside her wearing his tweed jacket, smoking his pipe, leaning towards her deferentially.

After the eggs Benedict, the flaky sweet rolls, the champagne and our third cup of coffee, Harvey walks us across the street to the Wyndham, and we invite him up to our suite. There, while he and Mother chat on the couch, Kitty and I withdraw. When they part, they hold each other for a long time, wanting to preserve the moment, knowing full well they might never see each other again. As things turned out, they never did.

Lucy in the small garden behind 58 West 8th Street, 1988.

"*I have had so many happy days, so many lovely days in my long life. And you will too.*"

So Many Lovely Days

I never know you now
Except when, like an Easter,
You branch along the dayspring of my veins
A total, telling impulse
Up, out of memory's cartoons.—Ray Smith

Branching along the dayspring of my veins, up out of memory's cartoons, is the last day I spent with Mother, October 15, 1994. A nursing home staff member had phoned to say they feared she could die any time now. Her temperature was dangerously high and a staph infection had invaded her body. The next morning, on the flight from Duluth, Minnesota to Atlanta, I read Stephen Levine's *Who Dies?* preparing myself for the ritual: massage the hands, rub the feet, give them permission to leave this life, wish them safe journey. As I sipped coffee, I popped a tranquilizer into my mouth.

I was glad Kitty was at work that soft, summery day. I wanted this to be *my* thing. Her kind husband, Dick, met me at the airport, let me stop at a florist—an old habit I couldn't break—and dropped me off at Cumming Manor. I went directly to room 104, prepared for the worst, but all I saw was the empty, carefully made bed. Anything but that! My heart pounded as I rushed to the nurses' station. I shouldn't have stopped for the violets.

Another shock. For there a woman in Mother's favorite outfit—purple velour pants and top—sits dozing in her wheelchair. Who is that small, bent woman? She holds a pad of lined yellow paper, on which someone has written with a marker: "My name is Lucile Dvorak Kirk. I live in room 104, Cumming Manor." It is Mother, ninety-six, short-term memory gone, incontinent, confined to a wheel chair for two years now. I kiss her and whisper in her ear: "Hi, it's your favorite daughter."

I always wanted to be her favorite.

Startled, she jerks her head up and opens her eyes, "Oh Kitty, I'm so glad to see you."

"You don't know how that breaks my heart," I say. Our old routine, but this time I'm not sure she recognizes me.

She reaches for the violets, her favorite flower, and yet so unlike her, and asks: "Did you come to take care of me?" smiling that sweet smile, her eyes now bright with fever. I love those shining eyes, and think of Shakespeare's wonderful words: "Age cannot wither her nor custom stale/ her infinite variety." But age *has* withered her. Terribly.

I want to say I came to help her die, but can't get the words out, and I'm afraid the "old" Mother will surface and say, "I have no intention of dying, Mary. You were always so difficult and willful." "Yes," I say. "I came to take care of you." I wheel her into the lounge where the bitter woman with the amputated leg, smoking in front of the blaring TV, doesn't acknowledge our greeting.

I catch my reflection in the lounge mirror, startled to see Mother's face of thirty-five years ago. I'm glad about that. "Be proud," she used to say, "of the high Dvorak forehead. Never cover it." I don't. I have Daddy's white hair and Mother's eyes, but we see things so differently now. Although she loved Roosevelt and refused to cross picket lines, as she aged and became more conservative she voted for Reagan, and supported the Vietnam "conflict." I'm wearing the light blue jumper I love for traveling ("too pastelly" says my daughter, Jenny), with purple blouse and socks in Mother's honor. How cruel to have a mirror here, I think, but then realize it's too high for wheel-chair-bound residents.

I wheel Mother back to her room. They no longer bother fixing her hair, which lies loose around her shoulders. I comb it gently, marveling that it's still brown, tie it back with a fuchsia ribbon ("like a dancer," I say,) and rub Tiger Balm on her bone-thin neck and shoulders. She, who always aimed to get under 140, now weighs less than 90 pounds. "Oh, that feels so good, Mary, don't ever stop." My heart sings: she's recognized me and remembers my old name.

"How about some ice cream?" I ask. Mother nods her head. I find the carton labeled "Kirk" in the residents' refrigerator and dish up some mint chip, her favorite. When I offer to feed her she purses her lips and shakes her head, no. So I tuck a napkin under her chin and hold the dish while she carefully, oh so carefully, feeds herself.

I softly sing a Cole Porter song that we'd played many nights on our baby grand in Manhattan and later in Pelham, "I get a kick every time I see your smiling face before me," and miraculously, her eyes smiling, her "eggshell voice" joins in, "I get a kick though it's plain to see/ you obviously don't adore me." We move on to "You'd Be So Easy to Love," and "Every Time We Say Good-bye," she hums along, voicing every few words, and my voice cracks as I sing "Why the gods above me/ who must be in the know/ think so little of me/ they allow you to go."

At eighty Mother sold the Pelham house and moved to an apartment in Atlanta to be near Kitty's family. After Mother's first fractured hip, my daughter Jenny kept her out of a nursing home by living with her for several months. Then, until her second fall two years ago, she'd played the piano daily. Or so she said. She also said she took walks daily in the nursing home. I never know quite what to believe. She doesn't exactly lie; she just no longer differentiates between inner and outer reality.

I rub Tiger Balm into her cold feet, noting how swollen and purplish they are, careful to miss the ugly gaping lesion that exposes her left ankle bone. "Doesn't this hurt you?" Her head is drooping. She's asleep. Miraculously, she's free from pain. I have a fleeting fear as I touch the oozing sore. Could it infect me?

I massage her fingers, noting how similar her hands are to mine, with veins close to the surface, and thin skin. I'm not glad about that. Her rings are now in the safety deposit box: things have a way of disappearing here. I remember how she convinced Daddy that she deserved a diamond. Not that she ever needed him to accede to her. She did as she wished. In her diary for 1952, their twenty-fifth anniversary year, she crossed out "bloodstone" as the birthstone for March and substituted "diamond." She knew her worth.

She opens her eyes. "What's happening to me?" I can't respond, and turn my face away to hide the tears. I put my arms around her, feeling it will help keep her from slipping away. I thought I was ready, but I'm not. I rub her shoulders, recalling a time of long ago. "Do you remember that summer I was eighteen, when I worked as a nurses' aide and gave you back rubs?"

She was fifty-four that summer of 1952, the Metropolitan, Travel, and Beauty Editor of Parents' Magazine. *With upswept hair, wide brimmed hats, trim suits, silk stockings and high heels, she attended Broadway plays, concerts, museum openings, and cocktail parties. As Metropolitan Editor she had to know what was going on in New York. She didn't have much time for her family. I determined not to be like her, to be more selfless, more loving, to put family first.*

That was the summer Daddy sipped soup because he had his remaining teeth pulled—one week uppers, the next week lowers. The summer he read Shelley, the summer he quoted over and over again:

> *Rarely, rarely comest thou,*
> *Spirit of delight.*
> *Wherefore has't thou left me now*
> *Many a day and night?*

Depressed and unemployed, he died of colon cancer within a decade. No more affairs for him. That summer Mother wrote in her diary: "Does valor pay? Does optimism?"

As I wheel her to dinner, Mother rallies and exhibits her old social skills. She smiles at a slovenly nursing attendant and says to her: "However old you are, you look ten years younger." I can understand why Mother was voted "Miss Cumming Manor." At dinner she wants to sit with Mary, a new resident, a former teacher, now deaf. Mother thinks Mary's an old friend from the *Cleveland Press* days, and gently touches her arm: "Yes, Mary was a first-rate reporter, the only other woman on the *Press*. Weren't those the days?"

"What's your mother saying? I can't hear a thing," says Mary.

"She had the handsomest brother," Mother continues, oblivious. "All us girls were crazy about him. Do you remember, Mary?"

Mary's full attention is on her food. She picks at the hamburger patty, ignores the potatoes, but butters the white bread with great care before dipping it into her tea. Mother leaves her meal untouched, but sips her tea, warming her ever-cold hands on the mug, and waits for more ice cream. I unwrap a Mr. Goodbar and split it between them. Only bacon, ice-cream, and candy taste good to Mother now. Never again her favorite dinner of roast pork loin with Pepperidge Farm dressing, mashed potatoes, sauerkraut, pumpkin pie, and André champagne, our standard fare for festive occasions.

It's becoming evident that Mother's death is not imminent. I'm shocked to realize this disappoints me. I so want to be with her at her death. Kitty, as Mother's primary caregiver, has been unstinting in her love and attention to her. Mother took Kitty to Bermuda when she was a teenager, and took two of Kitty's sons on European trips, but didn't take me or my children. Probably this was because she disapproved of my marriage to Ray, but still....Two years after Grandma Ada's death at 101, Mother chose to move from New York to Atlanta rather than to Duluth. But who's counting?

Her shriveled breasts sag. They used to be 36C. I always envied her. Once, when she was nursing Kitty in their fourth floor Village flat, she'd been startled to realize a man on the street was watching her intently with his binoculars. Sunday mornings my parents stayed late in their room. We had explicit instructions not to disturb them. I knocked anyway, and occasionally tried the locked doorknob. Then Daddy, whistling, took a shower, and Mother "washed up" and in their robes they came down to brunch smiling. "They still do it," I told Kitty. I used to think if a couple had *that* all other problems would fade away.

"Oh Mary, I'm so tired," says Mother, holding her head in her hands. "I could sleep forever." Does she know? I wheel her into her room, and call for the nurses' aides who unstrap her from the chair and lift her onto the egg crate mattress. How could those thin loins have borne Kitty and me? I close my eyes as they change her diaper, and remember Mother on an Easter day at our house in Pelham.

Upswept hair, purple ceramic earrings, lavender dress with a bright pink apron, a violet corsage, Mother greeted friends and international students from Teachers' College, where she'd earned her Master's of Education. Kitty (dark "like her father") and I (fair "like her mother") with Chanel #5 dabbed behind our ears, wearing pearls, cashmere sweaters, and ballet slippers, took their coats. Then we served the layered sandwiches we'd learned to make in Home Economics: cream cheese with olives and pimento, egg salad, tuna salad, on white bread with the crusts cut off. Delicious and so pretty, said our guests.

Mary, Lucy, George, Grandma Ada, Kitty; Christmas, 1946.

Daddy, whistling in the dining room, happily mixed martinis for the men, Manhattans for the women. He made a fire and then selected the music carefully, maybe Haydn quartets or Chopin—"nothing too intrusive—remember it's only background music," said Mother, who never loved classical music as he did. Grandma in the kitchen basted the pork, mashed the potatoes. Usually she was too tired to eat with us.

After dinner, that long ago Easter, someone played the piano and we sang the old songs; always "Annie Laurie" because of Daddy's Scottish heritage, and "Songs

My Mother Taught Me," because Anton Dvorak was Mother's paternal great uncle, or so the story went. (In 1993, at the Dvorak Centennial in Spillville, Iowa, I learned this was probably not so. "As far as we can tell," Dvorak's grandson told me, "no descendants emigrated to the U.S.")

I start to weep at the contrast between that warm house in Pelham and the sterile nursing home; between that laughing girl in pearls and cashmere and the white-haired woman in the blue jumper; between that hostess of long ago and the gaunt woman sleeping in the fetal position. She'll never again call me by my childhood pet name, "Marioka," never again tell me how she loves me. Her body is fully involved in the process of dying. In her last letter to me, she wrote: "I have had so many happy days, so many lovely days in my long life. And you will too." I hold on these words.

I think of the fortune teller who told Mother at eighteen that she was going to experience everything there was in life. Mother was ecstatic, determined to live her life fully. At ninety-two, after her fall, Mother said, "You know, dear, I didn't know she meant the bad too!" Yes, the bad too.

Standing by her bed, listening to her shallow, peaceful breathing, I recompose myself. Although I spent the first half of my life trying not to be like Mother, in recent years I have tried to change; like mother to be valiant and optimistic, to "warm both hands before the fire of life." I stroke her hot, dry forehead and kiss her goodnight. "Momma, you've been a most wonderful mother, my favorite. I love you so very much. Safe journey." I press her hand against my wet cheek, kiss it, adding, "I'll see you in November," knowing full well that it might not be so. And it was not. Eleven days later, on October 26, 1994, Mother died peacefully in her sleep, they said, but alone.

Maybe I, after all, have inherited Mother's rose-colored glasses, and will continue to see only what I want to see and remember only what I want to remember.

Epilogue: What Thou Lovest Well Remains

It has been twenty-four years since that evening on Mother's gold couch in Atlanta, sipping champagne and eating stale crackers and cheese, the evening I said to myself, "Someday I'll write about this." Daddy has been dead for forty years, and Mother for eighteen. I am not a daughter who visits her parents' graves. Daddy's ashes are scattered in Long Island Sound, and Mother's are buried in Cleveland's Lakeview Cemetery, next to her parents and her maternal grandparents.

Kitty, now eighty and in Atlanta, plagued by Parkinson's and recovering from a broken hip, may permanently require assisted living. (After we were widowed we had hoped to spend our last years together, but that dream did not materialize.) And I, sitting here in my Duluth home, surrounded by books and my beloved cats, am fast approaching my seventy-ninth year. I remain a bookseller's daughter—no Nook, Kindle, or I-pad for me. And I love my parents and sister now more than ever.

That long ago evening several questions puzzled me: why was Mother unkind to Daddy most of my growing-up years? Would they have been able to keep the book shop, and have a carefree, happy life without children? Can I ever make sense of their lives?

Reading Mother's diaries of the book shop years has answered several of my questions and has considerably altered my opinions about the romance of owning a book shop and about my parents. Do I now fully understand them? No, not by any means, but perhaps full understanding of others, much less of one's parents, is never possible.

For the majority of my adult life I felt that owning a book shop, especially in Greenwich Village, was the most romantic thing a person could do. It was my dream to replicate this experience myself and recapture the carefree Bohemian life my parents lived in the 1930s.

Mother's diaries have dispelled this myth forever. Although the book shop years were interesting, intense, and volatile, they were seldom romantic and never carefree. Because of my father's laconic, unreliable ways, lack of business acumen, unwillingness to assume responsibility, and alcohol dependence, the book shop was doomed from the start.

With the addition of a circulating library and seasonal greeting cards, Mother tried her very best to keep the shop going, but even these efforts failed to bring in sufficient income. Add to this mix two unexpected children, their illnesses, and the depression years, and it becomes a wonder that the shop stayed open for twelve years.

I very reluctantly have had to face some difficult truths about my father. Although he was an erudite, kind, and generous man, he was absolutely unwilling to be hemmed in by Mother's (society's?) rules. He never really grew up and he certainly never grabbed on to life the way Mother did. Although he almost always fell short of her expectations, I never gave up hoping he would change. But he never did. It amazes me that Mother stayed with him. She wanted to be in charge, wanted things her way, felt she deserved better, and she probably did. Aunt Scottie was right about him: he was a person who let things happen. And she was wrong about him also: although he was deeply flawed, he was not a drunken bum.

Mother loved life and had an extraordinary capacity for delight. An extrovert, she was confident, smart, and pretty. She expected the best from herself, her husband, and her girls. She treated her many friends well. She was a career woman, rather than a woman who centered life around her family. Although we children were not her top priority, she was a loving, responsible, kind mother. I regret not being more understanding of her during much of my lifetime and for blaming her for Daddy's alcoholism. I was ignorant. Aunt Scottie was right about her on both counts: she was a person who made things happen, and she was a wonderful woman.

And I? Do I remain my father's daughter, or have I become more like my mother? Have I become a woman who makes things happen? Perhaps only time will tell.

Do I understand my parents any better than I did years ago? Yes, somewhat. Will I continue my story about growing up in Greenwich Village where my parents owned a second-hand book shop? Truth be told, I have very sketchy, confused and jumbled memories of those years. Will I face the indisputable facts: I was less than six when the book shop closed forever, and during those first five years Kitty and I spent considerable time with our grandparents in Cleveland. No promises. Maybe I, after all, have inherited Mother's rose-colored glasses and will continue to see only what I want to see and remember only what I want to remember, whether it really happened or not. Ezra Pound was right: what I love well will remain; it will not be reft from me.

New York Addresses of George and Lucy

(All in Manhattan unless otherwise stated)

Cornish Arms Hotel, 315 West 23rd Street, March 7, 1927

58 West 8th Street, March 15, 1927

53 West 11th Street, October 1927

Elmsford, New York, summers 1928, 1929

632 Van Courtland Avenue, Yonkers, October 1929

364 West 11th Street, May 1930

19 West 8th Street, January 1931

111 Waverly Place (Margaret Freeman's), August 1931

364 West 11th Street, September 1931

216 Thompson Street, June 1932

111 Waverly Place (Margaret Freeman's), July, August 1932

45 Charles Street, January 1933

32 King Street, August 1935

Delaware Water Gap, Pennsylvania, summers 1936, 1937, 1938

20 W. Westminster Road, Brooklyn Heights, October 1937

13 Charles Street, September 1938

51 East 10th Street, September 1939

457 West 123rd Street, August 1940-August 1945

1 Hillside Avenue, Pelham, New York. (first house), August 1945-

[Note: In 1978, at eighty, Lucy sold the Pelham house and moved to 3200 Lenox Road, Atlanta, to be near my sister, Kitty.]

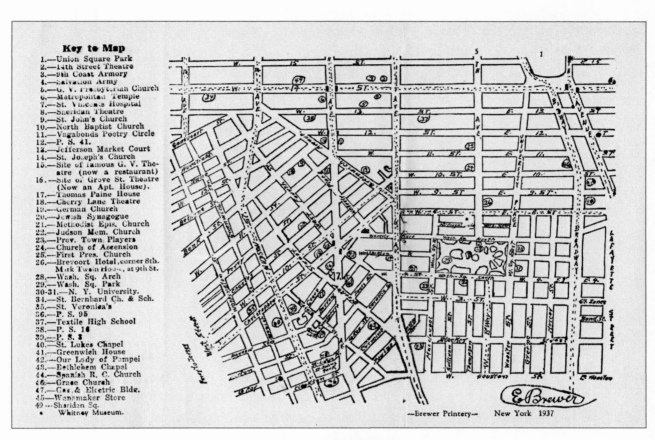

Key to Map

1.—Union Square Park
2.—14th Street Theatre
3.—9th Coast Armory
4.—Salvation Army
5.—G. V. Presbyterian Church
6.—Metropolitan Temple
7.—St. Vincent's Hospital
8.—Sheridan Theatre
9.—St. John's Church
10.—North Baptist Church
11.—Vagabonds Poetry Circle
12.—P. S. 41.
13.—Jefferson Market Court
14.—St. Joseph's Church
15.—Site of famous G. V. Theatre (now a restaurant)
16.—Site of Grove St. Theatre (Now an Apt. House).
17.—Thomas Paine House
18.—Cherry Lane Theatre
19.—German Church
20.—Jewish Synagogue
21.—Methodist Epis. Church
22.—Judson Mem. Church
23.—Prov. Town Players
24.—Church of Ascension
25.—First Pres. Church
26.—Brevoort Hotel, corner 8th.
    Mark Twain House, at 9th St.
28.—Wash. Sq. Arch
29.—Wash. Sq. Park
30-31.—N. Y. University.
34.—St. Bernhard Ch. & Sch.
35.—St. Veronica's
36.—P. S. 95
37.—Textile High School
38.—P. S. 16
39.—P. S. 3
40.—St. Lukes Chapel
41.—Greenwich House
42.—Our Lady of Pompei
43.—Bethlehem Chapel
44.—Spanish R. C. Church
46.—Grace Church
47.—Gas & Electric Bldg.
48.—Wanamaker Store
49.—Sheridan Sq.
•   Whitney Museum.

--Brewer Printery--   New York 1937

Map of Greenwich Village, 1937
by Eddie Brewer (Harvey Brewer's father)

ABOUT THE AUTHOR

Mara Kirk Hart, writer, editor, and life-writing coach, has published memoirs in poetry and prose and co-edited three periodicals and two anthologies. Her first book, *Lovecraft's New York Circle*, co-edited with S.T. Joshi, was published in 2006 by Hippocampus Press, New York.

Her beloved children and grandchildren live in Boston. She lives with two cats and many books in Duluth, Minnesota.